BUILDING WEALTH

A DIY Guide to Investing, Rehab Projects,
and Legacy Planning for your Graduate

Building Wealth

©2024 Marcia Castro-Socas

Published by Clovercroft Publishing, Franklin, Tennessee
ClovercroftPublishingGroup.com

Cover and Interior Design by Marcia Castro-Socas

Printed in the United States of America

ISBN: 9781956370607

Dedication

To my parents, for teaching me to work hard and think harder.

To my husband and children, for supporting me through all of the real estate adventures, conversations, investments, and renovations. Thank you for allowing me to immerse myself in what I love, and thank you for allowing me to both teach it to you and learn more with you.

Table of Contents:

Introduction

Investing

Chapter One: *Laying the Foundation for Wealth.*
Investing Early for a Baby's Mortgage-Free Future

Chapter Two: *Blueprints for Investment Success.*
Analyzing Properties with a Young Investor

Renovating

Chapter Three: *Renovation Roadmap.*
Renovating a Property With a High School Graduate

Introduction

If you wrote a book, what would the title be?

If there was something that you wanted to share with others, something that you knew because you lived it and loved it; how would you package this all into a few words that would convey it perfectly to the world? There's so much that you want to fit into the title, so much that you want the reader to grasp by just glancing at a book cover.

Would you choose a short, eye-catching title, or a longer one that encompasses everything that you hope to pass on? I thought through this over and over again, but when it came to naming this book, my main goal was clear.

It's about **Building Wealth**.

However, there's more to it than that, and I'm passionate about it, which led to the perhaps-too-long subtitle: A DIY Guide to Investing, Rehab Projects, and Legacy Planning for your Graduate. After all, I really wanted the title to reflect what's inside, the passion that I feel about building wealth through real estate and the stages that truly excite me— like investing in that great property, adding value to it through renovations, and ultimately building a legacy of wealth to pass on to my children.

There are other aspects of the subtitle that are perhaps not so clear…

Why is this a DIY Guide?

I've spent my share of time scrolling through DIY tutorials— whether it's to renovate a room, fix a household problem, or find the perfect recipe. What I love about good DIY tutorials is that they show you a whole picture. You get to see an entire process from start to finished product completed from start to finish. You see first and foremost that it *can* be done, and you learn from someone else's real-life experience—complete with all of the missteps, tips, and tricks they've picked up along the way. You see what worked, and why, and what they'd do differently to make it easier the next time. Most importantly, you witness the results.

That's exactly what I wanted to provide with this book. Real estate investing isn't just about theories and textbook strategies—although you need those foundations and they'll be provided here. But it's also about real experiences, real decisions, real adjustments, and real planning. I've chosen to share true experiences from my life because I genuinely believe that there's value in learning from someone else's journey. I want you to see the details of the transactions, the successes, and the unexpected. Plans don't always go perfectly, and that's okay. It's nothing to be afraid of, in fact, it's normal.

Now, I'll be honest—laying out my finances and investments for all to see isn't the easiest thing. But I genuinely believe that sharing my true experiences can help you navigate your own path more confidently. I believe that there's immense value in learning from someone who's been through it.

There's a lot of hype that exists about getting rich quick, and a lot of noise out there promising that you can make millions overnight if you just "buy this course," "join that program," or shell out for another seminar; but that's not what this book is about. I'm here to tell you that nothing I did made me wealthy overnight. What I'm sharing with you is the slow and steady approach that actually works—one that I've lived and breathed over the years. My success came from persistent and deliberate investing, one attainable amount at a time, which grew and compounded over the years.

Throughout this book, I'll walk you through various investment strategies that have worked for me as I taught my son about real estate investing. You'll see firsthand the different paths possible to build real estate wealth, whether it's long-term investing for your baby, the steady income of rental properties, the thrill of fixing and flipping, or even setting up an Airbnb. I'll also touch on tax laws that help you keep more of your hard-earned money—like using a 1031 exchange to defer taxes, selling a primary residence after two years to benefit from the capital gains tax exemption, and setting up a corporation and utilizing section 179. These aren't tricks; they're tools. And you'll benefit from learning how to use them.

Here's another thing I love about DIY projects—they're based on wanting to understand and do something for yourself. If you're like me, that thirst for knowledge drives you to learn, to create, and to take control of your own destiny. Did you know that people spend millions of hours each year watching how-to videos on social media? And thousands of self-help books are published every year—all because we're eager to better ourselves, to understand more, and to take charge of our lives. That curiosity, that desire to take control of your destiny, is at the heart of the entrepreneurial spirit. It's what drives us to learn, to grow, and ultimately, to succeed.

That force has transformed ordinary individuals into icons of financial success. Think of Andrew Carnegie, who started with nothing and built a steel empire that made him one of the wealthiest men in history. And we've all heard of Ray Kroc, who took a small chain of burger stands and turned it into the global phenomenon known as McDonald's, revolutionizing the real estate industry along the way by securing prime locations that became the foundation of his fortune. This same spirit drove Barbara Corcoran, who, with a modest $1,000 loan, built a real estate empire in New York City, proving that the right investment at the right time can change your life forever. It's not just about the money—it's about the vision to see opportunities where others see obstacles, like the college town Airbnb you'll read about. It's the courage to take calculated risks, and the determination to turn those risks into rewards. That same spirit that leads you to want to learn, that entrepreneurial desire inside of you, is what propels you to buy that first property, to renovate a space and see potential where others see problems, to build a portfolio that secures your financial future and creates generational wealth. History is filled with stories of those who harnessed this spirit to build fortunes from the ground up, often starting with little more than a dream.

Now, it's your turn to embrace that spirit, take action, and to start building your legacy. It's not just about huge achievements; it's about the courage to take that first step, to envision a future that doesn't yet exist, and to shape it yourself. No matter where you start, this spirit is within you, waiting to be ignited. It's the quiet whisper that says, "You can do this," and the fire that propels you forward even when the path is uncertain. History is filled with stories of ordinary people who harnessed this desire to achieve extraordinary things. That's the same spirit that fuels this book. It's about empowering you to take control of your financial future, to build something that not only benefits you but also your children and grandchildren.

Finally, let's not forget the satisfaction that comes with DIY. I can tell you from personal experience, there's nothing quite like the feeling of finishing a DIY project—whether it's a home renovation or, in this case, building a real estate portfolio. A few years ago, I decided that I wanted to take charge of my kitchen. My stove has a tile backsplash area behind it, and it was plain (and boring), just small beige tile which held no appeal for me. I'd lived with it that way for 15 years, as if it was my only option. Finally, one day I decided that this was my kitchen, and I had a right to make it look like I wanted it to. We removed the small beige tiles, and then I personally installed large blue and white bold and beautiful Spanish tile. I measured everything, spread the mortar, placed the tiles, and grouted it myself. Now, every day that I walk into my kitchen, I'm happy with what I see. It used to be "the kitchen". Now it's "my kitchen". Taking ownership and creating something I love has made all the difference. When you see the results of your hard work, when you've transformed something into something better, there's an incredible sense of empowerment-- there's nothing quite like stepping back and admiring your work. That's what I want for you through this book. I want you to finish it feeling inspired, confident, and ready to take on your own wealth-building journey.

Why "for your graduate?"

So, why "for your graduate?" Now, don't get me wrong—this guide is for investors of all ages.

I've included detailed explanations of essential real estate investing strategies for those who are just starting out, along with a section at the end of every chapter called "You," which offers actionable ideas to kickstart your journey. But I chose to incorporate "for your graduate" into the title because this process of investing in the particular properties in this book was something I did with my son, working to create a legacy and build wealth not just for him, but with him. When I looked back on the path that we took, I realized that major events and investments happened to coincide with ages in his life: infancy, 8th grade graduation, high school graduation, college.

I realized that throughout his life his education not only involved what he learned in school, it also involved an education in real estate investing, and that every project allowed him to graduate and advance to a higher level and new lessons. I was thrilled to have been able to participate and help him along in those lessons, building wealth along the way. And that's something I wanted to share with other parents and grandparents who are looking to do the same. That's why every chapter ending also includes a section with a few ideas of what parents or grandparents can do to help an investor on their way, whether that comes in the form of money, a loan, co-signing on a mortgage, or providing guidance and financial education.

Financial education is crucial—for our youth, for ourselves, and for the generations to come. I hope that this book contributes to that education, helping others gain the courage and confidence to invest and DIY your way to wealth. Yes, you'll need experts and professionals like realtors and accountants along the way (it's not all solo DIY), but at the end of the day, it's about recognizing that you hold your future, and the future of your descendants, in your hands. You can take charge, make it happen, and leave a lasting impact. You've got this.

So, let's dive in. Get ready to learn, to grow, and to DIY your destiny. Together, we'll explore the world of real estate investing, learn from my experiences, and start building a future that's not just financially secure, but full of possibilities. You're about to embark on a journey that could change your life—and the lives of those who come after you. Thank you for letting me be a part of it.

---

*Note: This book comes with worksheets, formatted for printing on letter sized paper, to help you. These can all be downloaded, for free, at: www.MarciaSocas.com/free-building-wealth-book-worksheets

---

The Worksheets
Goal Setting Worksheet
Property Evaluation Checklist
Investment Analysis Worksheet
Financing Options Comparison Sheet
Renovation Budget Planner
Property Management Checklist
Deal Comparison Worksheet
Monthly Cash Flow Tracker
Tax Deduction Tracker
1031 Exchange Worksheet
Exit Strategy Worksheet
Legacy Planning Worksheet

Chapter 1
Baby Steps

Laying the Foundation for Wealth. Investing Early for a Baby's Mortgage-Free Future

The Unexpected Advice

It was an ordinary day, the kind where you are completely unaware that a major change lies just ahead. My mom and I were in the car heading to see a property. It was a typically hot Florida afternoon, and the air conditioner struggled to keep the car cool. My mom sat in the driver's seat, her short hair styled perfectly as always, not a strand out of place despite the heat. We often drove together as we went to potential real estate listing appointments or researched an area for a client. We enjoyed our time together, talking about family, real estate, current events, but mostly about my son Eric. He was, after all, my firstborn son and their first grandchild. So, everything he did was met with the analysis and pride of a first-time parent and grandparent. Today, we talked about future plans.

My son Eric would soon be approaching his second birthday, and I didn't have a college plan set up for him yet. I couldn't see how I could have; after all, I had just come out of a large amount of post-divorce debt and was single-handedly renovating the fixer-upper home that Eric and I were living in.

I was working in real estate, which was not the path I had originally anticipated for my life. I was also divorced, another aspect of my life that was certainly not part of my original plan.

As we drove past the rows of houses, my mom turned down the radio, which had been softly playing in the background.

"So, have you thought about Eric's college plan yet?"

I sighed, glancing out the window at the homes we passed. "I've been thinking about it, but I haven't set anything up yet. With everything going on, I just haven't had the time—or the money, really. I was considering a prepaid college plan, but it feels like such a huge commitment right now."

I knew I had money for the college fund. A large portion had come as a gift from my parents, and some that I had in savings from his baby shower, Baptism, and birthdays. I just hadn't gotten around to pulling the trigger on the college plan and writing a check for the lump sum payment.

She looked at me a bit longer than she should for a driver who was supposed be focused on keeping her eyes on the road. "You know, there might be another way to secure his future without locking all that money into the Florida prepaid college plan."

I turned to her, curious. "What do you mean?"

"Well," she said, "instead of putting that money into a college plan that just sits there in the state's bank account for the next 15 years, why not use it as a down payment on a rental property?"

I wasn't sure I was following: "A rental property? But how would that help pay for college?"

"Think about it. If you buy a rental property, the tenants will pay rent every month, right? You can use that income to cover the mortgage and, at the same time, pay the monthly installments on the prepaid college plan. That way, you're not only paying for his education, but you're also building equity in a property that could eventually be mortgage-free by the time Eric graduates."

I thought through what she was telling me. At that time, the option for me for prepaid college plans was limited to the Florida prepaid plan. You could pay in one lump sum, or you could make monthly payments into the plan so that your child's college would be fully paid for by the time they went. You were essentially locking in future college fees at today's prices. The money went to the state, for their use, and you had the reassurance and peace of mind that tuition was paid for.

> Today, 529 plans are more popular. They weren't really used in the same way back then. Now, you can pay into a 529 plan every month and that money gets invested into the stock market, growing as time goes on. I love this plan because the money grows and you can use it for any school and for school related expenses, rather than being limited to your state school.

If I used all of the savings and gift money that I had for Eric, I could put a down payment on a house and then use the rental income to pay the college plan on the installment plan. And I'd still own the house.

"Exactly," she said. "You're turning that money into an asset, something that will work for you. And by the time Eric is ready to go to college, you'll have paid for his education and paid off the mortgage on a property that could continue to provide for him—maybe even give him a home of his own when he graduates."

The idea was revolutionary to me. I had always thought of money as something to be saved and used, something finite. But here was my mom, showing me how it could be used as a tool, something that could multiply and grow if handled wisely.

"Wow, I never thought of it that way," I admitted, feeling a new sense of possibility.

Like many of the things in my life at that point, this wasn't the path I had originally considered. I was focused on the traditional route—save money, buy a college plan, and ensure that Eric's education was secured. But my mom's idea planted a seed in my mind, one that grew into a new understanding of how money works.

Lesson 1: The Mindshift

This conversation was the beginning of a significant shift in how I viewed money and investing. It was the moment I realized that money shouldn't just be seen as the end goal but rather as a tool—a resource that, when used wisely, can work for us.

Investing requires a significant mindset shift.

Most of us are taught to save money to spend later, whether it's on education, a car, or even a vacation. But what if, instead of spending it directly, we invested it in something that could generate income? This way, we could still achieve our goals while allowing the money to grow and work for us over time.

The traditional way of thinking is:

Earn money $\longrightarrow$ Buy the thing I want

But now I was realizing that I could use the money to buy an asset (the house) that would generate cash flow that I could use to purchase the prepaid college plan:

Money $\longrightarrow$ Asset $\longrightarrow$ The thing I want

And, the best part is that the asset (the house in this case), continues to consistently generate cash flow every month. And while it's doing so it also goes up in value.

I started to think of this asset like a little engine. It provides an output (cash flow) but then also gets stronger and bigger as it works. It becomes more valuable as its own value increases over time, and as it gets bigger and more valuable it provides even more cash flow output. Rather than working to make money, this provides a way for money to set up an asset engine that makes money for me.

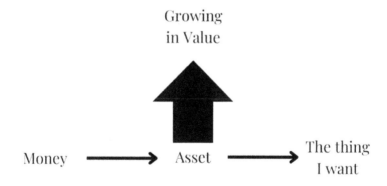

This house would be an asset, my little engine. It was a tool that would generate passive income and help me fund Eric's education while also building equity for the future.

The Deal

About the home:

It was a solid block construction single story home with a traditional shingle roof. The home had tile flooring in the main areas, and carpet in the bedrooms. The kitchen was simple but comfortable, and there was a fenced in back yard. There was also a small single car garage.

The home was listed at $88,000. I do realize that, at this point, you may think to yourself, "Well, of course, if I could find a house at $88,000, I'd buy it too". Pricing is certainly vastly different these days. But remember, this was back in 2003. So, the pricing seems incredibly low.

This should actually serve as a bit of revelation; after all, 20 years from now someone will be looking back at today's pricing and feel the same way.

It's like that famous quote by Ray Brown that states, "The best time to buy a home was always 5 years ago." *The next best time is now.*

How the deal was structured:

Purchased at $90,000

Even though the house was listed at $88,000, I offered the sellers $90,000 for the house and asked that they pay my closing costs. The closing costs at the time were approximately 3% of the price, so they paid around $2700 toward my closing fees, leaving them with $87,300—not far off from their list price. They accepted the offer, and we were under contract!

An Aside: *Wait, what are closing costs? (and how did you get the seller to pay for them?)*
Closing costs in a real estate transaction refers to the money that you must pay to get the closing completed. These include fees to the bank, government, title company, and sometimes homeowners' associations. I'll go over these in more detail in the Appendix if you'd like more information on these. You can ask sellers to pay toward your closing costs. How much they are allowed to pay is limited by your particular loan, but know that this is a valuable way to save upfront costs. More on this in the Appendix as well.

In Summary:

- Home listed at $88,000
- Sales price of $90,000
- The seller paid for my closing costs (approx. 3% charge to them)
- My commission as the real estate agent on the deal was $2,700, which I combined with the savings and gift funds I had for Eric to put together the down payment.

So, my payment amount looked like this:

Principal and Interest payment $570
Property Taxes and Insurance $250

Total of $820

If you're wondering how to estimate your monthly cost for a property, you can calculate what a mortgage payment would look like using this helpful calculator.
https://marciasocas.com/**building-wealth-resources/**

I secured a tenant for the property who was paying $945 per month. *I know that you can't find a house these days for that kind of rent but remember this was back in 2003.*

The net profit was $125 per month.

This is a small number. Smaller than most investors would recommend. Typically, I hear them recommend a profit of $250 per month so that you can build reserves for repairs.

But this was 2003, and $125 per month seemed like plenty to me and the home inspection had indicated no major issues that I was worried about. So, I wasn't going to let someone else's benchmark of what I "should" make every month stop me (and you shouldn't either).

And so it started.

How Real Estate Investing Starts to Build Wealth

Every month the tenant paid, the mortgage went down just a little, and I had an automatic draft set up to send the approximately $65 per month to the Florida prepaid college account. Slowly, I started building up a little cushion in my new 'investment property' bank account.

By the way, I can't stress enough how important it was for me to set up a separate account for those funds. If I had put that money into my account, I would have definitely ended up using it. Money was tight and it would have been easy to spend. But the fact that it was in a separate account, which I knew was growing for my son, and which I could see inching upward every month, was really motivational. It doesn't cost anything to open a second account, so just do it, and you'll feel differently about that account.

In this way, I was able to get the Florida Prepaid account going, and I only had to pay it in installments. Meanwhile, the rent I received from the tenant was going toward paying off the mortgage and the house was growing in equity.

So, the account where I had the $125 of rental income accruing every month then had an automatic monthly deduction of $65 per month. Leaving the monthly income at a whopping $60 per month. **But, the house was gaining in value, the mortgage was being paid down every month, and his University was being completely prepaid!** Totally worth it.

Could things have gone wrong? Yes, real estate investing has risks. There could have been expensive repairs or a non-paying tenant. However, the tenants were screened well and there were no major issues with the house. Well, there was one plumbing leak under the slab years later, but it was covered by insurance. They even paid for some new flooring in the house. I did have my own personal savings that I was working on in case this house needed anything, but fortunately I didn't need to draw on it. The little account started to grow bit by bit.

Now, since my little asset engine was producing even more than I needed for the prepaid college plan, my diagram started to look like this:

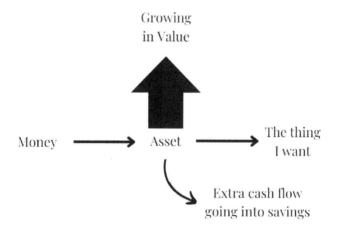

This was a wonderful strategy. Over the years, rental rates increased but my 30-year fixed mortgage payment stayed the same. I was able to store up a cushion of funds so that I would have it ready when repairs were necessary. Once there was more than I needed in reserves, I started sending in extra payments to pay down the mortgage faster. It was like a snowball effect, getting better year after year. By the time Eric was ready to go to college, I'd have the 4-year university tuition prepaid college program paid for, and before he reached the age of thirty, I'd have a home, free and clear, to gift to him.

"By learning to think differently about money, we transform it from a ruler into an instrument. Through education and practice, we become skilled players of this instrument, using it to acquire assets that work for us and build a legacy of wealth."

The little bit of down payment money that was originally invested into the house would eventually grow to a value of over $350,000 (at the time of this writing) and a prepaid college education.

The wisdom that my mother imparted to me that day about investing, and how you could make money work for you, opened my eyes, and created a valuable asset. That lesson changed my life and set me on a new path to investing, creative thinking, and a legacy of wealth through real estate.

Through this book I hope to show you where that lesson led me over the subsequent years. providing guidance, imparting a mindset, and helping you create a legacy for your children and grandchildren that will change their lives.

By the way, here's a look at the old price sheet for the Florida Prepaid University Tuition Plan back in 2001.

Tuition Plan Prices

Prices shown are rounded up to the next dollar. Actual payment amount may be slightly less. The application fee is not included in the prices shown. Prices are effective until January 25, 2002.

4-Year University Tuition Plan				
		120 Undergraduate Credit Hours		
Current Grade/Age	Projected Enrollment Year	Lump-Sum Payment Plan	Five-Year (55 Months) Payment Plan	Monthly Payment Plan
11th	2003	$7,836	$ —	$ 434
10th	2004	7,820	—	275
9th	2005	7,805	—	204
8th	2006	7,789	165	165
7th	2007	7,773	164	139
6th	2008	7,757	164	122
5th	2009	7,742	164	109
4th	2010	7,726	163	99
3rd	2011	7,711	163	91
2nd	2012	7,695	163	85
1st	2013	7,679	162	80
K	2014	7,664	162	76
Age 4	2015	7,648	162	72
Age 3	2016	7,633	161	69
Age 2	2017	7,618	161	66
Age 1	2018	7,602	161	64
Infant	2019	7,587	161	62
Newborn	2020	7,572	160	60

To purchase a new tuition plan, just complete the enclosed Enrollment Application. There is a $42 nonrefundable application fee to purchase a new tuition plan. There is no additional fee if you sign up for a local fee plan and/or a dormitory plan, for the same child, at the same time. The deadline is Friday January 25, 2002!

Source: college-bound-2001.pdf (itppv.com)

Lesson 2: The Power of Assets and Passive Income

When I was 10 years old, my parents worked in hotel administration. As you know, hotels are a 7 day a week / 24 hour a day kind of business; so, it wasn't at all unusual for my parents to work Saturday mornings.

Many Saturday mornings I could be found sitting in the arcade room of the hotel surrounded by the glowing screens of Joust, Q-bert, Pac Man, Centipede, Donkey Kong, and Galaga. I loved them all; but my favorite, by far, was Ms. Pac-Man. I would feed quarters into those machines by the fistful as I chased high scores and new levels.

My dad would say, "OK, here's twenty dollars' worth—come back when you need more." It wasn't that we were wealthy and that he was ok with me spending large amounts of money on games; in fact, quite the opposite. My parents were constantly working, juggling long hours to keep my brother and me in private school while striving to get ahead. The reason my dad didn't mind giving me what seemed like an endless stream of quarters was that he *owned* the video game machines.

He'd had the brilliant idea to contract with the various hotels they worked with, and he committed to supplying the video games to the properties in exchange for the arcade room space to put them in. The hotel could now advertise having a 'game room' without spending any funds to create one. My dad made the initial investment into the cost of the machines, and every week I would watch him take that small round metal key and remove the lock that held the metal strap that covered the front panel of the coin slots. Once the metal strap was moved, the panel door could be opened. Inside, under a mass of circuitry and wires, were the containers that held the quarters that had been dropped into the machine that week.

Sometimes he'd let me collect the quarters and bring them up to the office. I'd reach my hand into the pile of quarters and let the money fall through my hands. Do you remember those old cartoons with Scrooge McDuck and that immense treasure trove of coins he would dive into? Well, when I ran my hands through the bag of quarters, that was my Scrooge McDuck moment. I felt like the richest person alive. I'd carry the bag up to my dad's office, watch him set the coins into the coin sorter, and run back down with handfuls of quarters to play with until he was finished with his office work for the day.

What I didn't realize at the time was that this was really my first exposure to an asset, and the idea of how an asset can generate more money than it cost. My dad's video game machine costs were a fixed upfront investment, but those bags full of quarters kept churning out week after week. He had those arcade games for years, generating income and serving as a little engine pumping out money in the form of passive income. At the end, my dad still owned the machines, the original asset, which he could sell, and he'd made all of the money generated week after week.

You can see at this point how buying an asset differs from buying a final "thing." An asset continues to provide money in the form of passive income. At the end you have both the passive income and the original asset with its own value.

If you just buy a "thing," whether that be clothes, golf clubs, cars, or the college prepaid plan from the last section, that "thing" doesn't generate any more money. It decreases in value as you use it. But an asset is so much more. It works for you and generates steady cash flow. If you can use your money to buy an asset rather than buy the final "thing" you want, then you can use the cash flow from the asset to buy the "thing" and you still have your asset-engine churning out money for more things (and more assets!).

Isn't there a better term than "thing"?

I realize that the use of this generic term seems simplistic, but I think that "thing" really epitomizes that ultimate product that we want to buy. It can take many forms, and you might feel differently about that object depending on what it is. For example, if I were to say that the "thing" you're planning on buying is a car, some might call it a liability while others might say it's a depreciating asset because at the end of your use you do still have a car that you can sell, albeit at a lower value. Rather than get into semantics about liabilities or depreciating assets, I prefer to keep it simple and refer to that final object as the "thing." Because really, the focus here is not on the definition of the "thing" but rather the best way to buy it (with an asset and the generated cash flow).

I think that for most of us, we've been trained to believe that if we work for money, then we should be entitled to immediately purchasing the fun things that money can buy us. However, if we shift our thinking and just add in the asset-engine into our process, then we can start to see how adding this step can result in so much more than we originally planned for. If you use your money to buy assets, then you can use the cash flow from those assets to buy the fun items, and you can do it over and over again, rather than just once.

While real estate is by far my favorite asset, it isn't the only one that exists. Like my dad with the arcade games, there are other items you can buy that will generate income, sometimes you just have to open your mind to the idea and think about where you can implement it. For example, right now I own an older quadplex in Tampa that doesn't have laundry hookups in the individual units. We're thinking of investing in a couple of pay laundry machines to put into a spare storage area on the property. These would serve as a benefit to the tenants who live there and would also serve as an asset to us as we generate income from the pay machines. This would be a benefit to the tenants, avoiding them having to go to the laundromat. It would be more convenient for them and having an on-site laundry facility would improve the marketability of the quadplex in the future. The washing machines and dryers would be the asset, generating steady monthly cash flow. *Luckily, these machines run on credit cards now, making it even easier to collect the funds without having to go and pick up the quarters every week!*

In the case of buying the investment home for Eric's education and future, the rental income from that first asset was more than enough to cover the monthly payments for Eric's college plan. The extra money went toward creating a small savings for repairs and also contributed to paying down the mortgage more quickly by sending in extra payments.

That home was originally paying out only $60 per month (after the college plan payment). But it was consistent, and rental rates increased over time. Right now, that little asset engine generates over $552 per month in passive income. The tenant who lives there has been there for many years, so her rent is lower than the market rate, but she truly takes care of the home as if it's her own. That little asset-engine keeps creating more passive income, and the asset keeps growing in value.

By the way, even though my dad did eventually sell the arcade games, he did let my brother and I each keep our favorite machines. After all, a lot of the Saturday mornings in our childhood were spent with them. It's more than 40 years later and I still have my Ms. Pac Man machine in our game room. When we have a party, I turn it on and add a bunch of free credits to it, so that all of the kids can play on it. It still works, it's still my favorite arcade game, and I still hold the high score in my house.

Lesson 3: The Wisdom of Time in Real Estate

One of the most common concerns people have when considering real estate investment is timing the market. Many people worry about buying at the "wrong time" and want to wait for prices to drop. But the truth is, trying to time the market perfectly is nearly impossible and often leads to missed opportunities.

In my story about the home I purchased for Eric's education years ago, I didn't mention what interest rates were at the time. It also didn't matter if it was a buyer's market or a seller's market. The only things that really mattered, when looking back, were that the home could be rented without incurring additional expenses, and that the rent could cover the mortgage (and the college prepayment plan).

Now, that's not to say that educating yourself as to whether it's a buyer's or seller's market at the time of placing an offer on a home isn't important. It definitely is, because it will help you negotiate wisely at the time of your purchase.

How do you know if it's a buyer's or seller's market?

There are some indicators that you'll look for, or ask your real estate agent about. One easy one is the housing inventory in your area. Another is how long properties are typically staying on the market. When properties are under contract within days or weeks of being listed, you'll know that it's a seller's market. Additionally, when searching in a specific local market, looking at the list price to sales price ratio will show you if homes are generally selling at (or above) asking price, or if it's common for pricing to be negotiated.

Seller's Market	Buyer's Market
Low Inventory	High Inventory
Low days on Market	High days on Market
Multiple offers are common	Properties have no other offers
High list price to sales price ratio	Lower list price to sales price ratio

You will see in the table above that if there's high inventory and the property has been on the market for a while and doesn't have any competing offers on it, that property would lend itself well to an offer at a lower price because it's a buyer's market.

Once you have this information, you can put it to use by structuring your offer to best increase your chances of negotiating the price without missing out on the property. For example, if inventory is high and the property has been on the market for a while and doesn't have any offers on it, that property would lend itself well to an offer at a lower price. Additionally, you may be able to negotiate some seller paid concessions and closing costs that would save you money when it comes to closing.

Conversely, when it's a seller's market and you have a lot of competition for homes, your negotiation strategy will be different. It has always been helpful for me to try and ascertain what motivates the seller aside from price. For example, when there are competing offers on a property, I speak with the seller's agent and ask if the seller has an ideal time frame for moving. Would my offer be better received by them if I gave them two weeks after closing to move from the home? Would they prefer a very quick closing? Are they counting on the funds from this sale to buy another home—because if they are, then maybe what they want is a strong sense of assurance that I'm not going to cancel out of the deal and I can make them feel more comfortable with a large deposit. Obviously, price will always be a big factor for a seller, but even in a seller's market you should know that it's not the only factor. You can make your offer stand out in a variety of other ways, if you can just get an idea of what is important to that seller.

Knowing if you're negotiating in a buyer's market or seller's market is very helpful when presenting your offer and negotiating the best price and terms that you can. But, don't let the fears and predictions from opinionated friends saying that "prices are sure to drop," or "it's a bad time to buy," deter you from getting started with investing.

Over the past 30 years, real estate values in the United States have consistently risen. There have been dips, of course, but overall, the trend has been upward. The average home price in the U.S. has more than tripled since the early 1990s. This growth demonstrates that even if you buy at a peak, the value of your property will likely increase over time.

Now is always the best time to buy, because while property values may fluctuate in the short-term, they generally rise in the long term. This principle of equity growth is one of the most powerful aspects of real estate investment.

Federal Reserve Economic Data (FRED): The Federal Reserve Bank of St. Louis offers a wealth of economic data, including real estate prices. This graph shows the median sales price of homes in the US over time. (source: <u>Median Sales Price of Houses Sold for the United States (MSPUS) | FRED | St. Louis Fed (stlouisfed.org)</u>)

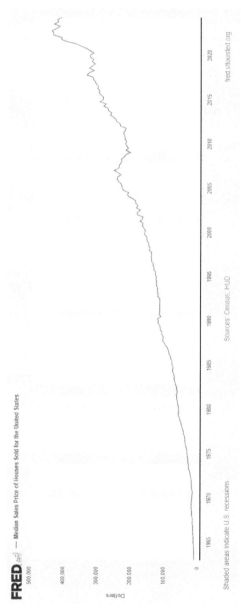

Lesson 4: Understanding Amortization and the Power of Extra Payments

Another key financial lesson I learned from this experience is how amortization works and how making just one extra payment per year can dramatically reduce the life of a mortgage.

Amortization is, simply, the paying of the principal and interest owed on a mortgage. The word originates from the Latin "admortire," which means "to kill." Essentially, with each payment you make you are killing off that debt.

An amortization table is a tabular way of seeing the payments on a loan. It indicates the monthly payment, and shows how that payment breaks down into principal and interest over time. The way that mortgages are structured, you pay primarily interest at the start of the loan.

Let's take a look at part of an amortization table as an example.

This is based on a $150,000 loan at 6% interest over 30 years:

Payment number	Payment	Principal	Interest	Balance
1	$899	$149	$750	$149,851
2	$899	$150	$749	$149,701
3	$899	$151	$749	$149,550
4	$899	$152	$748	$149,398
5	$899	$152	$747	$149,246
6	$899	$153	$746	$149,093
7	$899	$154	$745	$148,939
8	$899	$155	$745	$148,784
9	$899	$155	$744	$148,629
10	$899	$156	$743	$148,473
11	$899	$157	$742	$148,316
12	$899	$158	$742	$148,158
13	$899	$159	$741	$147,999
14	$899	$159	$740	$147,840
15	$899	$160	$739	$147,680
16	$899	$161	$738	$147,519
17	$899	$162	$738	$147,357
18	$899	$163	$737	$147,195
19	$899	$163	$736	$147,031
20	$899	$164	$735	$146,867
21	$899	$165	$734	$146,702
22	$899	$166	$734	$146,536
23	$899	$167	$733	$146,370
24	$899	$167	$732	$146,202
25	$899	$168	$731	$146,034

The amount going toward the principal is quite low, while most of those initial payments are set up to go toward the interest portion of the loan. At this rate, when you're finished paying the mortgage at the end of 30 years, you will have paid a total of $173,757 in interest. That's in addition to the original $150,000 that you'll pay off. (Total payments of $323,757 over the life of the loan).

Now, if you make one extra payment each year, applied directly to the principal, you can cut the mortgage term down by several years and save you thousands of dollars in interest. This strategy accelerates the process of building equity in your home, allowing you to pay it off more quickly and increase your wealth. Here's how our amortization table looks when we make one additional payment per year:

Payment number	Payment	Principal	Interest	Balance
1	$899	$149	$750	$149,851
2	$899	$150	$749	$149,701
3	$899	$151	$749	$149,550
4	$899	$152	$748	$149,398
5	$899	$152	$747	$149,246
6	$899	$153	$746	$149,093
7	$899	$154	$745	$148,939
8	$899	$155	$745	$148,784
9	$899	$155	$744	$148,629
10	$899	$156	$743	$148,473
11	$899	$157	$742	$148,316
12—extra here	**$1,798**	$1,057	$742	$147,259
13	$899	$163	$736	$147,096
14	$899	$164	$735	$146,932
15	$899	$165	$735	$146,767
16	$899	$165	$734	$146,602
17	$899	$166	$733	$146,436
18	$899	$167	$732	$146,268
19	$899	$168	$731	$146,101
20	$899	$169	$731	$145,932
21	$899	$170	$730	$145,762
22	$899	$171	$729	$145,592
23	$899	$171	$728	$145,420
24—extra here	**$1,798**	$1,071	$727	$144,349
25	$899	$178	$722	$144,171

With this strategy, not only will you pay off the loan more than 5 years earlier, but you'll also save thousands of dollars in interest charges. In this case you'd pay $138,305 in interest, a savings of $35,452.

I took advantage of this strategy throughout the years. At the end of every year I would look at the property's bank account, save a little bit for emergency repairs and reserves and send the rest in to the bank earmarked "for reduction of principal."

The balance of the loan dropped significantly, and I wasn't tempted to use those extra funds for anything else because I sent them in regularly and didn't allow them to accumulate past my set amount for reserves.

Also, when the interest rates dropped significantly, I did refinance the property. Doing so allowed me to lock in a lower rate and shorter time frame. I refinanced to a 20-year term at a lower interest rate, so my payment didn't increase, it actually decreased! I mention this because, while it's smart automate these payments and not think about the money coming into the account, you do need to also keep your mind on your rental business and keep your eye on advantages that you can take. *Remember, refinancing will involve closing costs, so weigh the cost to refinance against the amount of savings you will benefit from in order to determine if it's a good choice for you.*

How You Can Do This Too: A Practical Guide

You might be wondering how to take the first step into real estate investment, especially if you're just starting out. Here's how you can get started:

- **Save for a Down Payment:** The first step is to save enough for a down payment. Typically, you'll need at least 3-5% of the home's purchase price, though putting down 20% can help you avoid mortgage insurance and lower your monthly payments.
- **Explore Low Down Payment Options:** Look into programs that offer low down payment options. These programs can make it easier to get into your first investment.
- **Negotiate Closing Costs:** When making an offer on a home, consider asking the seller to pay for closing costs. This can reduce your upfront expenses and make it more feasible to purchase your first investment property.
- **Pay Attention to the Market:** Don't try to 'time the market' and wait to buy, but do remain aware of market conditions and how they might help you with your investment—like refinancing to a shorter term and lower interest rate.

Helping the Next Generation: How Parents and Grandparents Can Assist

Just as my gift funds for Eric helped me with my first investment, parents and grandparents can play a crucial role in helping their children or grandchildren get started in real estate. Here are a few ways to assist:

- **Provide a Gift for the Down Payment:** A financial gift can make a significant difference, helping young investors overcome the biggest hurdle to buying their first property.
- **Obtain the Loan:** If your child or grandchild is a baby, as in my example in this chapter, obtaining the loan yourself and placing it into a trust for your child/grandchild (I do own the home in the name of a Revocable Trust for Eric) would provide a future asset for them. You can also use some of the monthly cash flow to pay into a 529 college account so that money can grow and pay for their future college expense, while the real estate asset grows as well.

Conclusion: A Legacy of Wealth

Investing in real estate is more than just buying a property; it's about creating a lasting legacy of wealth that can support you and your family for generations. By making smart financial decisions, shifting your mindset about money, and focusing on building assets, you can lay the foundation for a prosperous future.

In the next chapters, we'll dive deeper into the practical aspects of real estate investing, including how to find the right property, manage your investments, utilize leverage, and continue building wealth. But it all starts with that first step—the decision to invest in your future, just as I did for my son.

Chapter 2
Elementary School

Blueprints for Investment Success. Analyzing Properties with a Young Investor

Time passed, Eric grew, and I continued to educate myself on real estate investing. I read books and listened to CDs about financial education while in the car; I also learned from clients who sometimes had me place aggressively (and embarrassingly) low offers. I was amazed when some of these "crazy low offers" led to them securing great deals! They all taught me to keep opening my mind to see potential deals and learn to negotiate a bit more effectively every time. I was now a full time Real Estate Broker, having purchased the company from my mom, and I was a part time investor, having purchased a few properties throughout the years and holding them as rentals. I had remarried, and my husband John and I often spoke about business (he owned his own company), investing, and real estate.

Eric loved conversations about business, and seemed to enjoy dreaming about how he would make money in the future. He would excitedly tell me about new ideas and inventions that he thought up; he'd imagine how he could make his plans come to fruition and how successful he would be.

So, it didn't come as much of a surprise when Eric sat us down one day and said that he needed to talk with us about investing. He was young, with big brown eyes, a deep dimple in his left cheek when he smiled, and a mouth full of braces. It was summertime, and we were sitting outside on the back porch when he sat down, a very serious look on his face.

"I'd like to talk with you guys about something," he began.

Immediately, we knew this was an issue that was important to him—there was no mistaking the intensity and focus he had. I put my phone down and gave him my full attention.

"What is it? Is everything okay?"

"Oh, yeah," he said, "it's just that I'd like to ask if I can use some money for something. Actually, it's my money I'd like to use, if that's okay."

"What do you mean?" I asked him. "Yes, if you have some money and want to buy something, that's fine. Do you need me to take you to a store later?"

"No, no," he continued, wanting me to hear him out and take him more seriously. "I want to know if I can use all of the money I have in my savings account."

He knew we had a small savings account for him. In it was money he'd received as gifts for birthdays or Christmas, or when my dad paid him for the A's and B's on his report card.

If he wanted to use all of this money, it had to be for a significant purchase. "Okay, honey, what do you want to buy with all your savings?"

"Well, you know how my friends and I love playing video games, right?..."

Over the next few minutes Eric explained that there was a game coming out that he and all of his friends were anxiously waiting for. This new FIFA game was going to have some extra feature and it's all any of the other boys his age were talking about. He was so convinced, and so passionate, that we decided that we would let him use all his savings to invest in it. We hoped it would be a good lesson on investing and how that can grow slowly and steadily over the years.

We took the $700 from his bank account, and told him we'd round it up to $1000 for him to invest because we were happy he was choosing to invest long-term rather than just buy something temporary.

We purchased stock in a company called Electronic Arts (EA) when it was approximately $12 per share. This was around July of 2012. Just two months later, in September, the demo of FIFA 13 was released and was downloaded a record setting *2 million times* over 3 days. The stock price rose steadily and checking the price became a hobby for us. By the following summer, in July of 2013, the price was up to a bit over $24 per share. *Eric had doubled his money in one year!* Over $2000 worth of stocks were now sitting in the account!

At this point I became a bit panicked. A mistake on my part for sure. I just couldn't envision how this could keep going up in value, and I became afraid that Eric would lose the money and hate investing. I told him we had to sell it. "Doubling your money in one year is enough, lesson learned, let's take the win and be happy. You did an amazing job investing."

I'm a bit embarrassed to admit it but, as I write this to you, that same stock is trading at $150 per share. I should have never had him sell it back then. I wish I'd found another way to give him back his earnings while silently keeping the stock money invested for him. But it was a different time, I let fear take hold and didn't want to become too 'greedy' and lose the earnings. And anyways, as I'm excited to tell you about in the upcoming pages, he had another plan for the money…

It all started with our ability to talk about money and investing at home.

Lesson 5: Let's Talk About Money

One of the most valuable lessons I have learned as a parent is the importance of making financial conversations a normal part of everyday life. Money is often considered a taboo topic, one that many parents shy away from discussing in front of their children. But in our home, we chose a different approach. We believed that by openly discussing investing and business, we could equip our children with the knowledge and confidence they'd need to navigate the financial world.

From an early age, Eric was exposed to conversations about real estate investing, equity, and the intricacies of renting homes and collecting rent from tenants. These weren't just abstract concepts—we talked about real deals we were involved in, the challenges we faced, and the strategies we used to overcome them. We wanted our children to understand that money isn't just something you earn and spend; it's a tool that, when used wisely, can help you build a secure future. By involving Eric in these conversations, we demystified the process of wealth-building.

Having these conversations also helped us. We found that by putting our goals into words, we would formulate our ideas. When we wrote this plan down, it became a plan, and by sticking to the plan we began to reach the goals we set.

"A dream written down with a date becomes a goal. A goal broken down into steps becomes a plan. A plan backed by action makes your dreams come true." — Greg Reid

---

There's a beautiful beach on the western coast of Florida that we travel to every year over the holidays. When we do, we always take a day to sit and review the performance of our investments. We also create goals for the next year in terms of growing our real estate portfolio and how we can meet our goals. This exercise has proven to be extremely powerful. I'd often heard of people saying that writing down your goals would make them more likely to happen. But I never really believed it, not until we started doing it ourselves and I saw how powerful and motivating it was to have clear goals to strive for. So, the conversations about investing were fantastic not only for Eric, but for us as well.

By making money and business topics part of regular conversation, we also fostered a sense of confidence and curiosity in our children. They weren't intimidated by financial matters because they had grown up hearing about them. Instead, they became curious—asking questions about how mortgages worked, why some investments were riskier than others, and what it meant to build equity. This curiosity is the foundation of financial education; it's what drives children to learn more, explore options, and ultimately, make informed decisions as they grow older.

There are several statistics and studies that highlight the positive outcomes for children who are taught financial literacy from a young age. Here are a few key findings:

1. **Financial Literacy and Adult Outcomes**:

   - A study by the **National Endowment for Financial Education (NEFE)** found that individuals who receive financial education are more likely to demonstrate improved financial behaviors, such as budgeting, saving, and avoiding excessive debt. These behaviors contribute to better financial outcomes in adulthood.

   - The **Council for Economic Education** reports that high school students who were required to take personal finance courses had higher credit scores and lower rates of delinquency on debt by the time they reached adulthood.

2. **Early Education and Long-Term Financial Health**:

   - According to a study by the **Brookings Institution**, children who are taught financial literacy from a young age are more likely to save money, budget effectively, and manage credit responsibly as adults.
   - The **Jump$tart Coalition** found that students who receive financial education in school have a higher propensity to save money, are less likely to use credit cards irresponsibly, and are more likely to invest in stocks and bonds as they grow older.

3. **Parental Influence and Financial Success**:

- A report by the **T. Rowe Price's Parents, Kids & Money Survey** revealed that kids who frequently discuss money with their parents are more likely to have a better understanding of financial concepts and make sound financial decisions as adults.

- The same survey found that 82% of parents who talk to their kids about money at least once a week report that their children understand the value of money better, compared to only 53% of parents who don't discuss finances regularly.

4. **Correlation Between Financial Education and Wealth Accumulation**:

- Research by the **FINRA Investor Education Foundation** shows that adults who received financial education in their youth are more likely to save for retirement, own stocks, and accumulate greater wealth over their lifetime.

- The **Global Financial Literacy Excellence Center (GFLEC)** at George Washington University has found that individuals with higher financial literacy are more likely to plan for retirement, which is strongly associated with greater wealth accumulation.

These statistics underscore the importance of teaching financial literacy at a young age, as it has a profound impact on the financial well-being and success of individuals later in life. I've included citations and links to these studies in the Appendix, in case you'd like to read more about any of them.

So here we were, with a little over $2000 and a great lesson learned in investing in stock. I was so happy with his outcome, but I was just nervous about the volatility the stock market could have. I would prefer if he try to invest in real estate. But could it be possible with this amount of money? What would be the right property to invest in? I needed to teach Eric how to analyze properties for investment.

Lesson 6: Analyzing Properties

It's summertime, 13-year-old Eric is working with me for the summer, helping me with mailouts and paperwork, and accompanying me to visits to rental properties that I manage. Today, I'm training him to evaluate properties and set aside his preconceived notions and biases and look at the numbers and see how we choose properties to invest in. We sit together, out on the back porch again, with a laptop and a notepad.

Below is his first assessment, and it shows clearly why you shouldn't bring your assumptions into real estate analysis.

I asked Eric to evaluate 3 properties:

- A townhome in an upscale neighborhood
- A single-family home in a working class neighborhood
- A townhome in a low-income neighborhood

But, before we started, he needed to call a lender and find out what qualifications are currently necessary for an investor to buy. It's important to double-check lenders' criteria, as these do change from time to time.

I had spoken with a lender I knew, and told her to expect a call from Eric. He wouldn't take more than 10 minutes of her time, but I wanted him to learn to communicate and ask these types of questions over the phone. She was more than happy to take the call and give him the information.

Here's what the lender told him a buyer needed in order to purchase an investment property:

- Minimum credit score of 700
- 15-20% down payment funds
- A debt-to-income ratio less than 45%

If he met those criteria, the bank could offer a loan at approximately 4.75%-5% interest rate for 30 years.

With this information, we could start analyzing the different properties. We decided to use a 20% down payment plan and a 4.75% interest rate for all of the properties analyzed.

(We did not include loan associated closing costs in our assessment, as we just wanted to look at a comparison between the properties without getting too much into closing costs and how to ask for closing cost credits)

Townhouse in upscale part of town (Windermere, Florida) *Eric's favorite*

We found a 1,500 sq ft townhome priced at $250,000 in a great part of town. Windermere is an area where many celebrities live and that you may have seen in the news for some high-profile stories. We found a townhome in the area that was competitively priced, and ran the analysis.

This was Eric's favorite property by far, he liked the look of it and the location, and liked the idea of owning a property in Windermere.

Here's how the monthly numbers worked out:

Expenses	
Sale Price	$250,000
Down Payment (20%)	$50,000
Monthly Principal & Interest	$1,043
Homeowner's Ins. (monthly) cost	$130
Property taxes (monthly)	$198
HOA	$360
Total monthly expense	$1,731

This townhome also had a homeowner's association fee of $360 per month which needed to be factored in.

Total monthly payment: $1731

We also looked at the recent rental rates in the area for similarly sized units to see what the rent income could be. It looked like we should be able to rent the unit for $1850 per month.

Total potential monthly rental income: $1850

This leaves a monthly gain of $119. This small margin means that your profit for months could be wiped out quickly so you'd need some savings on hand just in case.

Another thing to look at, for me, is what my initial cash investment is returning. In this theoretical scenario, we invested $50,000.

In the first year, assuming no repairs, the max profit we can make is
$119 x 12months= $1428

If we take the $1428 / $50,000; we see that our return on our initial investment for the first year is only 2.8%. You would do better to have the money invested another way, since the stock market and some savings pay a better return than this.

Income	
Potential monthly rent	$1,850
Monthly Net Income	$119
Max Annual Income: (12 X Monthly Net Income)	$1,428
Return on Investment: (Max Annual Income/Down Pymnt)	2.80%

Needless to say, Eric was disappointed. This exercise of analyzing real estate investments for passive income wasn't working out for the property he thought it would. His summary was:

PROS:

- Excellent area

CONS

- Expensive
- Not a great monthly income
- Not a good return on investment

Working Class Neighborhood Home

Our next analysis was on a home in the neighborhood I grew up in. The homes are from the 1970s, solidly built, they have good sized back yards, but they're nothing fancy. Just solid homes for hard working people. This is an area I like investing in quite a bit, in part because I grew up there and I like updating the houses and making them look good and provide a great place for families, but also because I think they're solid investments.

We found a 1,225 sq ft single family home for sale which actually looked pretty good because it had already had recent upgrades to some of the expensive systems. It needed a little cosmetic updating, but it was certainly rentable and could be easily updated (just some paint would go a long way) if we wanted to spruce it up.

Expenses on This Home	
Sale Price	$183,000
Down Payment (20%)	$36,600
Monthly Principal & Interest	$763
Homeowner's Ins. (monthly) cost	$100
Property taxes (monthly)	$159
HOA	$0
Total monthly expense	$1,022

On this one, the potential monthly Rent based on recent rentals in the area was $1400, so our income calculations looked like this:

Income	
Potential monthly rent	$1,400
Monthly Net Income	$378
Max Annual Income: (12 X Monthly Net Income)	$4,536
Return on Investment: (Max Annual Income/Down Pymnt)	12.40%

Monthly Net Income: $378

Now those are some better looking numbers!

Let's look at the return on the cash invested:

Our max yearly income is $378 x 12 = $4,536

Our down payment on this one was $36,600

If we take the $4,536 / $36,600; we see that our return on our initial investment for the first year is 12.4%. Much better than what we saw with the townhouse.

Eric's summary was:

PROS

- New roof, AC, and electric
- Block construction, house is sturdy
- Great return on investment

Low Income Area Unit

We received a call from a wholesaler who had a unit for sale at a great price. The unit is a bit far, about a 1 ½ hour drive which makes repairs a bit difficult because we don't know many repairmen in that particular area, but I asked him for the numbers so that we could see if it made sense.

The unit is around 1000 sq ft, so it's the smallest of the ones we analyzed.

Expenses	
Sale Price	$59,000
Down Payment (20%)	$11,800
Monthly Principal & Interest	$246
Homeowner's Ins. (monthly) cost	$100
Property taxes (monthly)	$53
HOA	$0
Total monthly expense	$399

Total monthly expense: only $399

We can get government subsidized (like Section 8) guaranteed Rent in that neighborhood for: $840 per month

Here's how our income calculations look on this one:

Income	
Potential monthly rent	$840
Monthly Net Income	$441
Max Annual Income: (12 X Monthly Net Income)	$5,292
Return on Investment: (Max Annual Income/Down Pymnt)	45.00%

That is the biggest cash return of all of them and it requires the smallest cash investment!

If we take the $5,292 / $11,800; we see that our return on our initial investment for the first year is a whopping 45%. That is seriously huge!

Suddenly Eric was getting more excited about this whole exercise!

PROS

- Beautiful return on investment
- Lots of cash in per month
- Lower down payment, more available to most people

CONS

- Far away and we don't know the condition

So, here's the summary of where we are, all in one chart after analyzing real estate investments for passive income.:

Price	$250,000	$183,000	$59,000
Down payment	$50,000	$16,600	$11,800
Monthly Expense	$1,731	$1,022	$399
Potential Monthly Income	$1,850	$1,400	$840
Potential Monthly Net Profit	$119	$378	$441
Max Yearly Return on Cash Investment	2.8%	12.40%	45%

What about an increase in equity over time?

Eric was disappointed and surprised that his favorite, the townhouse in the expensive part of town, wasn't the best one. But he was still rooting for it, so he asked a pretty interesting question at this point, and one that does play a part in analyzing real estate investments.

"Maybe you get more monthly rent from the lower priced properties, but I think the luxury townhouse will be worth more in the future."

It was really a very valid question, and I was impressed he was thinking of this long term as well as for the monthly cash flow. So, we decided to pull the statistics for the sales over the past five years in all of the areas and see how they looked. (I could do this because I'm a Realtor with MLS access and that made the statistical search really easy but you can also do this using online research and pricing estimates).

Here's what we found:

Data from upscale townhome area:

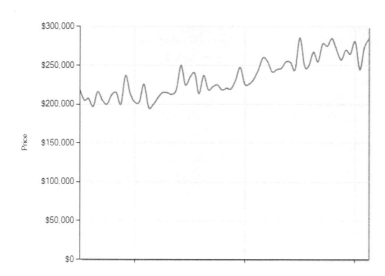

Over the past 5 years, the average price of a townhome in this area went from $205k to $285k, an increase of 39%

Data from modest area single family home:

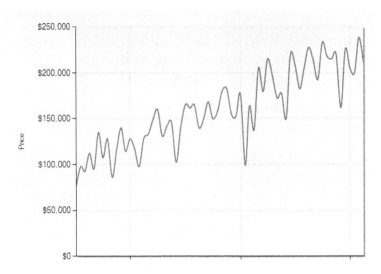

Over the past 5 years, the average price of a single-family home in this area went from $97,750 to $210k, an increase of 115%.

Data from low income unit:

When we tried to research the low income area, there simply wasn't enough historical data to produce a chart. While this isn't ideal, it is real life. Sometimes you may not be able to accurately assess everything you'd like to. However, we could see that, in the few published sales that we could find, there was not very much growth in value over the past 5 years.

Equity Summary:

Eric wanted to know why this would happen, because his gut instinct was that the townhome in the more upscale area would gain value most quickly. I think that part of why this happened is that when you start at a lower price point, there is a larger group of people who can afford that home, and so the increase is quicker and easier.

Also, a single-family home has greater demand and can fit more families' needs than a townhome, because traditionally in our area families prefer single family homes where they can have back yards for playsets and family bar b que's. Townhomes often just don't give the space some families crave. (This may differ in other areas of the country)

His Notes:

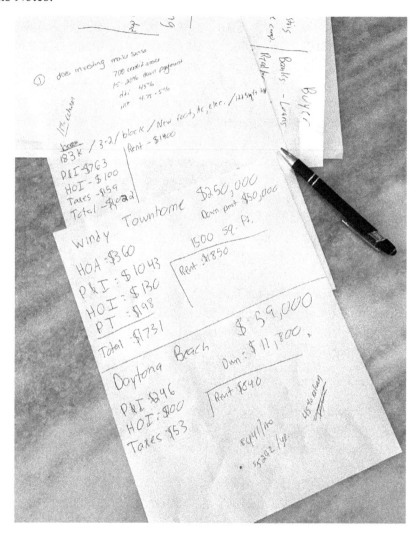

While this was a great exercise to show Eric that we need to run the numbers on an investment property, not go for the one we simply like best, it doesn't encompass everything that goes into the calculation you'd want to do when investing in a rental of your own. Let's add a few more components to it.

A more involved evaluation

In analyzing a property, you'll want to take into account some real-world risk factors that could reduce your income. The first one is the fact that you may have a rental property that is vacant for a period of time between tenants, or you may have an issue with a tenant who doesn't pay their rent. You will have some control over these elements, and screening tenants well, collecting adequate security deposits, and working on any late payments issues quickly will all help you keep down your potential losses in this area. However, they will always exist, and you should be aware of them and factor them into your property analysis. These items are generally known together as "vacancy and collection". I would estimate 5% for vacancy and collection, but others may estimate a bit higher, at 10%. You'll come up with a figure that feels comfortable to you, and that may also be based on whether or not the property is already tenant occupied when you purchase it. If you're purchasing a vacant property, you'll need to assume it will take you some time to get it rented. Hopefully you can work with the seller to start marketing the property for rental before you get to closing so that you can sign that lease right when closing is complete and start earning money right away.

The first step in evaluation would then be:

> Potential Gross Income (the max rent you can expect in a year)
> -Vacancy and Collection
> Effective Gross Income   *(Step 1)*

This is new, more realistic, expectation of yearly rental income. From this amount, you'll want to deduct your operating expenses. These are expenses that are associated with owning and maintaining the property. These are things like homeowner's association dues, property taxes, homeowner's insurance, lawncare, utilities, and repairs.

Calculating this, our next step becomes:

> Effective Gross Income (from the calculation above)
> -Operating Expenses (again on a yearly basis)
> Net Operating Income   *(Step 2)*

The Net Operating Income is an important number because, if you've noticed, we haven't taken out any expenses for our own mortgage yet. This Net Operating Income shows only the income and expenses associated with this particular property, regardless of what the size of our down payment was, what our interest rate was, or how much our particular payments are.

Now we will want to keep the calculations going so that we can see how our numbers will look with our specific mortgage payment. The next step is to take our mortgage payments (principal and interest) and calculate what they are for the year (just take the principal and interest and multiply by 12). This is also referred to as "debt service". So, here's where we are now:

Net Operating Income (from the calculation above)
-Annual Debt Service
Cash Flow Before Taxes   *(Step 3)*

Now we've taken everything into consideration and this Cash Flow Before Taxes is the actual amount of money you should expect to earn for the year.

This final formula looks like this:

PGI

-V/C

EGI

-OE

NOI

-ADS

CFBT

Congratulations! It's not always easy to get through that formula, but now that you have, you are equipped to assess the property, and you can also run several higher level calculations as well.

Let's run through an example:

Property price: $200,000
Down payment $10,000
Loan of $190,000 at 7% interest for 30 years
Anticipated rental rate for the area: $1800

Using the mortgage calculator I find that my Monthly Principal and Interest repayment on loan: $1265

PGI ($1800 x 12)	$21,600
−V/C (5%)	$1080
EGI	$20,520
−OE	$4,000
NOI	$16,520
−ADS	$15,180
CFBT	$1340

This property is generating a cash flow of $1340 and your initial investment was $10,000.

When we calculate $1340/$10,000 we can see that your return on your $10,000 investment is 13.4% in the first year. After the first or second year, you'll hopefully be able to raise the rent a bit, and your return on investment percentage will increase. Additionally, the tenant paying the rent is paying down the mortgage amount, and your investment should be increasing in value.

From this one set of numbers, you can perform higher level calculations. Some may be of importance to you, and others may not. I've included a spreadsheet where you can easily run this formula for a property, as well as see some additional investment calculations, at:

https://www.MarciaSocas.com/building-wealth-resources

So, what did we do?

The very low-income unit we analyzed presented the largest potential income stream; however, it was far away, and I didn't really feel that we could upgrade and maintain the unit the way I'd like to.

We decided that it would be best to focus on a property that was closer to home and in a bit better condition than the low income area property. Soon, we found a foreclosure deal on a townhome that was in a solid area (but not an expensive luxury area), in good condition, with a low HOA. It was 2 bedroom, 1 ½ bath, and we were able to purchase it at $75,000.

I asked Eric to put in a 3% down payment, which would be $2,250. He gladly put in his money from the EA stock and we helped with the rest of the funds necessary to establish a note and mortgage on the property.

We couldn't put a home in the name of a 13-year-old, but we wanted him to feel the ownership of the property. We had Eric think of a company name and he thought long and hard about it and came up with a name that he felt exemplified a company he'd like to run. We opened an LLC with the name he chose, which would allow us to keep the property separate from our other holdings. This way he would work for the company, with the idea being that we could transfer ownership of the LLC to him (along with the properties owned) in the future once he was over 18.

Eric in front of his first investment property on closing day—just a couple of months before 8th grade graduation.

Lesson 7: Leverage

Now that we're talking about getting loans for investment properties, it's important to discuss leverage.

Leverage in real estate refers to getting a loan (using debt) to purchase property. When you have money to invest, utilizing leverage can make your money grow exponentially faster.

Let's go through a hypothetical scenario to see how this works.

There is a transformative power of leverage—it is a tool that has turned countless individuals into millionaires.

Here's the question...

Given $100,000, what is better to do with the money? Would you buy one $100,000 house cash, or put five 20% down payments (assuming 30 year mortgage at a 5% interest rate) on $100,000 houses?

We will be analyzing the differences between these decisions after one year, 5 years, and 10 years. In both situations we will assume 7% equity growth on our properties.

We will have some constants in both scenarios:

All of these imaginary houses are in the exact same neighborhood. Each home in our example is therefore able to bring in the exactly equal Monthly Rental amount of $1200.
Taxes and Insurance are also identical in all our sample houses, but we will not ignore them. We will give them a cost of $200 per month for each house.

No HOA fees, and no theoretical repairs or vacancies to calculate. This exercise is to see what the same amount of money can do with and without leverage. Any real estate investment can have vacancies, collections, or repairs, but we will assume the risk of these is the same for all our hypothetical houses.

Now that we've got that straight, here we go into the analysis:

Purchase one house outright for $100,000 (no debt).

After **one year**, there will be a cash flow of $14,400 ($1,200 per month x 12 months). Our one house also pays $200 per month in taxes and insurance, which reduces our **cash flow to $12,000** per year.

There would be an equity growth of 7%, bringing the value of our investment at the end of year one to **$107,000 value.**

After **5 years**, there will be a **cash flow of $60,000** ($12,000 per year x 5 years).

The value of our home will be $140,255. How did we get that?

Remember that we are assuming property value goes up by 7% each year. So, at the end of year 1, the house is worth $107,000
at the end of Year 2 = $107,000 x 1.07 = $114,490 value
at the end of Year 3 = $114,490 x 1.07 = $122,504.30 value
at the end of Year 4 = $122,504.30 x 1.07 = $131,079.60 value
at the end of Year 5 = $131,079.60 x 1.07 = $140,255.17 value

After **10 years**, there will be a **cash flow of $120,000** ($12,000 per year x 10 years)

The value of the home will be $196,715 (continuing to calculate 7% per year growth)

So at the end of 10 years, we have a total potential **profit of $316,715**

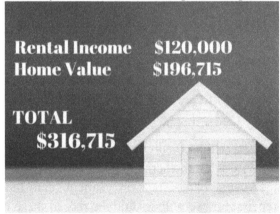

Next up, the five properties with mortgages.

In this scenario, rather than purchasing one home with our $100,000, we've decided to purchase 5 homes. In order to do this, we've had to get loans on the properties. We've put $20,000 down payment on 5 different homes. And we've gotten a loan for the balance. Essentially, it looks like this:

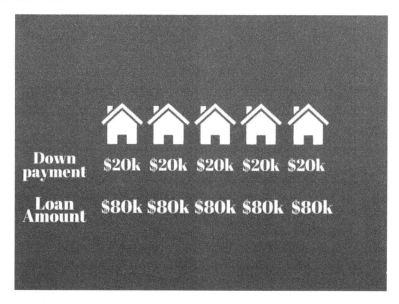

Now we own 5 homes worth $100,000. Each home has a loan on it that we have to repay. As we mentioned before, we are going to assume we obtain a 30-year loan at 5%.

Utilizing a mortgage calculator, we find that the monthly loan payment to the bank for each house will be $429/mo.

Our tax and insurance payment is $200 on each house. Therefore, each home has a **monthly expense of $629**.

The Monthly Rental Income is $1200 on each house, minus the monthly expense of $629.

That means that each home has a **monthly income of $571**. That's much less than our one home example, but remember, we own FIVE of these homes now. So, we need to take our $571 monthly income per house and multiply it by 5. **Our monthly income is therefore $2,855.**

After one year, there will be a **cash flow of $34,260** ($2855 per month x 12 months).

Now let's calculate our value of one property. Each home was worth $100,000 and went up in value by 7%, making it now worth $107,000 at the end of year 1. The five homes are worth $535,000 in value ($107,000 x 5 homes). (Although remember that if you sold these right now, you'd need to pay back the loan on each one so all of that money isn't yours right now).

After five years, there will be a **cash flow of $171,300** ($34,260 per year x 5 years).

What about the home values?

Just like with our single house, the home value went up to $140,255 at the end of 5 years. But this time we have 5 houses, so our **total home values are $701,275** ($140,255 x 5). But remember, we do still have outstanding loans on these properties.

After ten years, there will be a **cash flow of $342,600**, and now let's delve deeper into our home values and what this would really be worth if we were to sell at this point.

Just as our one home in the first scenario went up to a value of $196,715, so did each of our homes in this example. We have 5 homes, so we multiply $196,715 x 5 and get a value for our properties of $983,575. Now, let's assume we are really going to cash out at this point. We'd have to pay off those loans and see what we're really left with. One of the beautiful things about the loans is that we've been making payments every month from the tenant's rent, (remember the $629 we were sending to the bank every month?). Our loan amount has therefore been getting paid down little by little and now we don't owe $80,000 on each home anymore. We now owe $64,915 per house on each loan. Altogether, that's a loan debt of $324,575.

So now, our 5 homes are worth $983,575 but we need to pay off the total loan amount of $324,575. So, what we would actually keep of the **home's values is a total of $659,000**.

Combine this with our rental income of $342,600, and, using leverage, our profit has been **a whopping $1,001,600. <u>Congratulations you are now a millionaire in real estate!</u>**

Amazing, isn't it?

The same amount of money invested in Scenario 1 yielded you a total of $316,715, but over $1 Million in Scenario 2 where you utilized the power of leverage.

Lesson 8: Socially Conscious Rentals

Have you ever had someone approach your home, and you just instinctively know they're trying to sell you something? You want to avoid the conversation, but you also don't want to be rude. That's exactly how I felt one day when I saw a stranger walking up the path to my real estate office. I didn't have any appointments scheduled, and random walk-ins were rare, so I assumed this visitor was here to pitch me something. Anticipating a sales pitch, I reluctantly opened the door.

The woman who entered was well-dressed and polite. She asked if we handled property rentals.

"Oh, yes," I replied, "are you looking for a rental? We don't have anything available right now, but I'd be happy to take your name and number." Our rentals were fully leased, and I thought offering to take down her information would allow me to quickly return to my work.

"No," she said, "I actually wanted to talk to you about housing for the homeless."

Over the next 30 minutes, she introduced me to the organization she worked with, the Homeless Services Network (HSN). I had never considered leasing homes to the homeless and was initially concerned about how the properties might be maintained. However, she explained that each client in the program had a dedicated caseworker who regularly visited the home to ensure it was well-maintained and to coach the tenant on proper upkeep.

Section 8 is one of the most widely recognized programs, and while my experiences with it haven't been flawless, they've been overwhelmingly positive. The rent payments have always been timely, and the annual inspections by the Section 8 inspector have helped keep the property in good condition. But this HSN program was new to me, and I was interested in helping and loved that there was an active caseworker ensuring things went as smoothly as possible.

I spoke with Eric about the HSN program and the importance of helping others who need a hand up. We discussed how the funds were guaranteed by the program, ensuring that rent would always be paid on time and in full.

Charlie and Susan were the tenants placed through the HSN program, and after signing the lease, they moved in. Initially, I was in frequent contact with their caseworker, seeking updates as I adjusted to the program and their property visits. However, Charlie and Susan soon settled in and began to take pride in their home. When a hurricane swept through the area, we were fortunate to suffer only minor damage, mainly a few fence panels that came down. Despite the relatively minor damage, repair crews were unavailable due to higher-priority jobs in the area. We decided to handle the repairs ourselves, and Charlie stepped in to help us re-secure the fence posts and panels. During that time, Eric learned that Charlie had served in the military, and their conversation led to a deeper discussion later about how good people can face unexpected circumstances that lead to financial hardship and homelessness.

Susan eventually found work, and soon, Charlie and Susan were paying a significant portion of the rent themselves as they progressed through the program. Although our personal interactions with them were limited, it was incredibly rewarding to hear of their successes through the caseworker. Renting to them felt like more than just a business decision; it felt like we were genuinely helping someone with our property.

I share this story because I encourage you to consider renting to low-income program. These programs may vary from county to county, but they are worth exploring in your area to see if they work for you.

You: How you can start

- **Utilize leverage:** If you'd like to start utilizing leverage to grow your real estate empire, start by contacting a lender. You can learn so much in a 15-minute phone call. Ask what programs they have for investors, what the minimum down payment is, and what the interest rate is. If you don't like what they have to offer, contact someone else and see if they have any different loan programs. You can also search online for investor-friendly lenders who might have different options. For example, there are some loans that are based solely on the anticipated rental income of a property. These loans aren't based on your income at all, they're based on the rental's ability to cover the loan. They're called DSCR loans, if you'd like to look them up online and learn a bit more about them.
- **Educate yourself:** Continue opening your mind about investing and passive income, via real estate and other methods. There are great books and podcasts and lectures that will help you with this. I'll list some of my favorites in the Appendix section.

Legacy: How you can help your children or grandchildren start

- **Offer Guidance and Mentorship:** Sharing your knowledge and experience can be invaluable. Guide them through the process, helping them avoid common pitfalls and make informed decisions. Talk about money and investing, what you've done right and maybe even what you've done wrong that they might be able to learn from.
- **Take out the loan:** Eric wanted to get involved in investing but he certainly couldn't get a mortgage at the age of 13. Consider taking on the mortgage and overseeing the process for a young investor. It will give you the opportunity to have an investment together, teach them simple accounting as the rent comes in and the mortgage payment goes out, and will also be providing a wonderful asset for them.

Conclusion: Empowering the Next Generation

By the end of this chapter, I hope you see how early lessons in investment analysis and the smart use of leverage can set young investors on a path to success. Just like a well-designed blueprint is crucial for a building's structure, these financial principles are vital for creating a solid foundation for wealth. Teaching these lessons to the next generation isn't just about handing down knowledge—it's about empowering them to build their future.

Chapter 3
High School

**Renovation Roadmap.
Renovating a Property With a High
School Graduate**

Chapter Three: Renovation Roadmap: Renovating a Property with a High School Graduate

The high school years flew by, and soon we were ready for another graduation. We thought about what to give him as a graduation gift, but didn't know quite what to get him. We didn't want to get him something that would quickly go to waste, and there didn't seem to be too many sentimental gift items for boys (other than maybe a watch). However, around that time, I learned of a condo unit for sale in a gated community over by the airport. Once again, real estate presented itself and I was happy to move on to another lesson in real estate investing with Eric.

Rather than provide a traditional gift, Eric received a mortgage and title to a little one-bedroom condo. The down payment amount was the gift, but the mortgage was going to be his responsibility. The good thing is, the condo was being sold with a long-term tenant in place, so it was making money from day one.

The interesting thing about this condo is that I didn't find it on the MLS; I found it through a wholesaler, and the price was fantastic...

Lesson 9: What is wholesaling in real estate?

Have you ever received a random text or phone call asking if you want to sell your home? Even if you don't own a home, you may have gotten one of these messages by mistake.

This is from a wholesaler.

And then there are the cheesy get-rich-quick schemes you might have seen online. Flashy videos and courses claim that you can make a fortune in real estate without any upfront investment.

They want to sell you on the idea of wholesaling.

More often than not, these pitches are centered around the idea of wholesaling. They lead with promises of easy money, but the reality is far more complex.

If you don't know what a wholesaler is, here's the definition from investopedia.com :

In real estate wholesaling, a wholesaler contracts a home with a seller, then finds an interested party to buy it. The wholesaler contracts the home with a buyer at a higher price than with the seller, and keeps the difference as profit.

Generally, the reality of this situation is that you have a desperate seller who is in a situation where they need to sell quickly. The wholesaler provides them a way to get out of their home quickly, but at a low price. The wholesaler 'sells' this deal to an investor, who buys the undervalued (and typically distressed) property.

Understanding the Basics of Wholesaling

At its core, wholesaling involves three key steps:

1. Finding the property
2. Getting the property under contract
3. Assigning the contract

Finding the Property: The first (and most challenging) step is identifying a property that can be purchased below market value. Wholesalers typically target distressed properties or motivated sellers. Since I own rental real estate, I often get texts and calls from wholesalers asking if I'd like to sell a property. Many wholesalers use mass text systems to send out huge amounts of these texts; or they sometimes use overseas services to make the phone calls for them. Then if someone is interested, they schedule a follow up call with the actual wholesaler. The conversion rate for cold calls is generally quite low, with success rates typically ranging around 1% to 2%. This means that, on average, for every 100 cold calls made, only 1 to 2 might result in a lead that could potentially turn into a deal. So, while the flashy courses and videos may tout this as a 'no cost' way to get into real estate investing, realize that there is a value to your time and the process often requires significant effort, with wholesalers needing to make hundreds or even thousands of calls to secure a few contracts. You'll be reaching out and trying to find homeowners who are eager to sell quickly due to financial difficulties. Other reasons homeowners may be willing to work with a wholesaler is that they have an inherited property, which means wholesalers also scour obituaries and divorce filings, as well as other public records .

If this type of thing seems appealing to you, here are other places that wholesalers can find potential sellers:

Public Records: As mentioned, you can search probate listings, divorce filings, foreclosure records, or tax liens to find properties in distress. These records are usually available through county websites or the local courthouse. Once you have the listings and names, you can then obtain the owners phone numbers and addresses. If you don't know how to find them, you can utilize "skip tracing services" which find this contact information for you .

Driving for Dollars: Driving for dollars is the general term given for physically driving through neighborhoods to identify distressed or vacant properties. Wholesalers note the addresses and later use skip tracing services to find the contact information for the owners .

Real Estate Data Providers: There are companies that compile real estate data from multiple sources and sell that information to investors and wholesalers. There are several sites online that offer this service. These platforms allow users to filter properties by various criteria, such as equity percentage, property type, or owner's situation (e.g., absentee owners), making it easier to target potential sellers. If you'd like to see an up-to-date list of some of these providers with links to their websites, you can visit my resources section at:
www.MarciaSocas.com/building-wealth-resources

Networking: Some wholesalers build their contact lists through networking with real estate agents, other investors, and professionals in related industries. These contacts can provide referrals or inside information about properties that may not yet be on the market. They'll also help when it comes time to selling the contract on the property   .

Online Listings and Marketplaces: Websites like Craigslist, Zillow, or For Sale By Owner (FSBO) listings can also be sources of leads for wholesalers. They can identify properties that have been on the market for a long time or those listed by owners who may be more flexible on price.

Getting the Property Under Contract: Once a potential deal is found, the wholesaler negotiates with the seller to get the property under contract. The contract gives the wholesaler the right, but not the obligation, to purchase the property at a specified price within a set time frame. Importantly, the contract often includes a clause allowing the wholesaler to assign the contract to another buyer.

Assigning the Contract: Instead of purchasing the property themselves, the wholesaler finds an end buyer—often a real estate investor—who is willing to pay more for the property. The wholesaler then assigns the contract to this buyer and collects an assignment fee, which is typically the difference between the contract price with the seller and the price the end buyer is willing to pay.

The Appeal and Reality of Wholesaling

The appeal of wholesaling lies in its perceived accessibility, the "anyone can get started with real estate investing" tagline. With minimal upfront investment, wholesalers can potentially earn significant profits by leveraging their knowledge of the market and negotiation skills. This approach is often marketed as a way to "get rich quick" in real estate, which explains why so many online courses and seminars tout it as a golden opportunity.

However, the reality of wholesaling is more complex than it appears. Success in wholesaling requires:

- **Market Knowledge**: To identify properties that are truly undervalued, wholesalers need a strong understanding of their local real estate market. This way they can accurately assess property values, especially for distressed properties.

- **Strong Negotiation Skills**: Securing a property under contract at a price that leaves room for profit is not an easy feat. Wholesalers need to be skilled negotiators that can work with sellers who are typically involved in a stressful situation in their life.

- **Building a Network of Buyers**: In order to be successful, wholesalers need a network of cash buyers—real estate investors who are ready to purchase properties quickly. Building and maintaining this network is essential, as it determines how quickly and profitably a wholesaler can assign contracts.

- **Legal and Ethical Considerations**: Wholesaling exists in a gray area of real estate law. In some states, the practice is heavily regulated, and failing to comply with local laws can result in legal issues. Additionally, ethical concerns arise if wholesalers misrepresent their intentions to sellers or engage in high-pressure sales tactics.

Ethical Considerations

Personally, with regard to the ethical considerations, I've have never chosen to become involved in wholesaling real estate because I had always thought of it as a bit "shady". I also feel strongly that it would go against my code of ethics as a licensed Realtor to become a wholesaler. After all, wholesalers are trying to negotiate the <u>minimum</u> price possible with a seller. Meanwhile, as a licensed Realtor, I feel that it's my duty to always let a seller know what <u>maximum</u> price they can sell their property for. These two things seem in conflict to me, and I would never want to give anyone less than the best advice and service I can give them.

For a long time, I even refused to consider buying a home from a wholesaler because I felt that it must involve a seller who was being taken advantage of, and I just didn't want any part of that. But then, one day, I met a wholesaler who had a property for sale. I agreed to take a look at a property he had, one where the seller would be there.

The property was in disrepair and was being sold at a price that reflected that. The carpet was missing in about half of the property, the cabinets were old and a few of the doors were hanging loosely from the hinges. The bathroom needed a total overhaul, and there was moisture coming in around the window sills. The price still made this unit attractive. The seller was there (she had met us there to unlock the door). She seemed really happy about the sale, and I had always expected people who worked with wholesalers would be at an agonizing low point in their lives. She definitely didn't seem to be upset at all. I asked the wholesaler if I could speak with her, because I wanted to feel comfortable with the transaction. He said he was totally fine with it.

I approached her, wanting to understand but not wanting to say anything that might offend her, "So, I noticed that you're selling your property directly through Brian, and I'm certainly interested in it because I love properties that I can renovate. I'm just curious if you don't mind, what made you decide to sell this way?"

She answered, "This property has been in disrepair for a while, and I just don't have the time, energy, or money to fix it up. I had a tenant, but he's leaving, and I don't want to pay the association dues and other costs to keep up the property, I just want to sell it fast."

I still wanted to know more, so I pushed the envelope a little bit by asking, "I guess as a Realtor I always think people will want to put their property on the MLS and sell it that way. This is a new way of buying for me and I wanted to make sure it's something you're happy with."

She smiled at me and said, "Oh, I understand why you might think that, but for me, it's actually a relief to sell through Brian. He offered to buy it as-is, no questions asked. I know I'm selling for less than what the property might get if it were fixed up, but honestly, I'm okay with that, and I wish you the best with it if you want to put your time into that. I'm still making a profit, and for me, I don't have to deal with repairs, inspections, paying commission, paying fees while the property sells, or waiting months for a buyer to come along. Brian is offering a quick closing, and I'll have my money in two weeks. That's what I want."

I thanked her for being honest with me about her feelings and told her, "That's really interesting. I guess I never considered that some sellers might actually prefer this type of arrangement. My favorite part is the fixing but I guess it isn't everyone's favorite"

"Exactly," she answered. "For me, the convenience and speed outweigh the higher price I might get elsewhere. Brian isn't taking advantage of me; he's providing an option that fits my situation perfectly."

I kind of felt sheepish afterward. Because, really, it wasn't my place to have judged why people choose to wholesale a property, and not my place to have judged Brian either. This conversation definitely made me feel differently about the entire wholesaling process. I still don't feel that being a wholesaler is right for me, but I no longer judge the situation. I accept that it's right for some people and I'm happy to buy from a wholesaler who has a good deal available.

Challenges and Risks

While wholesaling can be lucrative, it is not without risks:

- **Finding Deals**: The market for distressed properties is highly competitive, and finding and negotiating a deal can be time-consuming and challenging. Wholesalers often spend significant time and money on marketing and outreach efforts to locate potential sellers.

- **Financing Contingencies**: Some contracts include contingencies that allow the wholesaler to back out if they can't find a buyer. However, if these contingencies are not well-structured, the wholesaler could be left with a contract they are legally obligated to fulfill, putting them at risk of losing their deposit.

Details of our condo deal from the wholesaler:

Going back to our situation, and the purchase of this condo as a graduation gift, you need to put yourself now in our position as the end buyer. This wholesaler had me on his email list, which is how I originally saw the property listing.

This wholesaler had a contract with the seller to purchase the property at $57,500.

He was charging us a wholesaling fee of $10,000 to purchase the contract. That made our price $67,500 plus we had to pay for all of the closing costs.

This was a great deal on the property, however there were some pretty strict stipulations.

In this type of transaction, there was:

- **NO inspection period**
- **NO financing (it's a cash only purchase)**
- **QUICK closing (14 days from contract to closing)**

So, this brings us to another important question. Is a condo inspection necessary for flipping?

Obviously, it would be scary to buy a home with no inspection, but remember this is a condo. The exterior and the roof are covered by the association. I scheduled with the wholesaler to meet him at the property and take a quick look inside. This particular property had a tenant inside, and a property manager overseeing the property, so the timing had to be coordinated so as not to inconvenience them.

Once inside, the property manager told me there had been a leak inside the unit. A pipe had burst in the wall but they'd already had a professional plumber come and fix it, and they had installed new carpet. The carpet was a regular brown cheap material, and I did get the contact info and warranty info for the plumber who had done the repair, just in case of a future issue.

The cabinets and bathroom looked ok. Not amazing, but there was a tenant in there who was happy and paying rent, and everything was in good working order. It just looked outdated. It's easy to see past that when you get used to seeing how easily things can be renovated.

The air conditioner was a concern, because that would be the biggest potential expense in a condo unit like this. It looked old, but it was running and pumping out cold air.

Buying a Condo with a Tenant in Place

The tenant wanted to stay in his lease, which for us was an added bonus. He was paying $895 per month and had 7 months remaining on his lease.

The property manager was charging 10% of the rent every month, so that was a fee of $89.50 per month. Although it would have been nice financially to terminate the property management agreement and keep that additional $90 per month, there are three reasons that we didn't.

1. It didn't seem right that this property manager had gone through and taken care of the unit and especially a unit that needed repairs, and that she would be dumped once she had finished taking care of those things.

2. The property manager was the one who had coordinated all of the repairs and she had a long working history with the plumber; so if something were to happen again, we felt that it would be most effective to have her demand that the plumber repair it correctly without extra fees.

3. She had a relationship with the tenant and he was paying well under her management and we didn't want to create waves in the payment relationship

We made an agreement with the property manager to keep her on until the end of the lease. That would give us 7 months to establish a relationship with the tenant and to make sure there were no further plumbing leaks.

How debt became Eric's graduation gift

We figured that the best gift we could give Eric was a great investment like this one. The other 1-bedroom units in the complex were selling, at that time, at an average of $80,000.

However, we weren't simply going to buy it for him as a gift, that would be ridiculous...

We were willing to gift him the "down payment" on the unit and we would finance it for him.

At a purchase price of $67,500, if someone were to get a loan with 3% down payment, their down payment amount would be $2,025 and they would obtain a loan for $65,475.

This $2,025 investment was going to be our graduation gift to Eric. But it came along with a mortgage payable to us for the balance. The mortgage was at 4% for 20 years.

So, essentially, our high school graduation gift to Eric was a mortgage in the amount of $64,475. It sounds pretty strange to give the gift of debt, but it came backed with a great condo and the opportunity to learn more about how investing works while acquiring another asset.

Eric was responsible for making the loan payments on time, and he was also responsible for keeping track of all income and expenses. This helped him learn to truly balance an account, write checks (or send online payments), and make sure that he paid bills on time.

Just two months into the lease, unfortunately, the a/c blower motor went bad. So much for my ability to judge an a/c by looking at it! The property manager handled the repair, and she also deducted the cost from the rental income.

After the 7 months, we already had a good history with the tenant, and we felt comfortable that there were no plumbing issues. We let go of the property manager (saving us $89.50 per month) and increased the rent to $950 upon the lease renewal. Now we had reduced an expense and also increased the income, the profit margin was already growing.

Lesson 10: When the Unexpected Happens

Eric graduated high school in May of 2019, and things were smooth sailing until the end of the tenant's lease, and several months into the renewal.

But then, in March of 2020, we had the Covid lockdown. So much was changing at that time, and things were so uncertain. In the months that followed, I worked with tenants as they cut back on work hours. I worked out situations with them where I allowed them to skip a rent payment. I told them we'd create an agreement to temporarily allow their security deposit to be used in place of rent and they wouldn't need to worry about replacing the security deposit funds until after all this uncertainty was over. Tenants were grateful and relieved, and I still had the rental income, and we were working together.

Eric's college closed due to the pandemic, and students were sent home. He completed his classes online while we all sheltered in place and waited for things to return to normal. Weeks turned into months, and school remained closed.

Unfortunately, the tenant in the condo was laid off from his job during this time. We worked with him as much as possible so that he could stay but eventually, by the end of June 2020, he had made the decision that he was going to move to another area, and he asked if he could break the lease. Of course, that was no problem with us. It would make no sense to try to force him to pay rent with everything that was going on. We created a mutual termination of lease agreement and wished him the best in his move. He left the property empty and clean, and paid his rent through the very last day he was there.

So now here we were, with an empty unit. Eric had a mortgage to pay, and there were association dues that needed to be paid every month as well.

One look at the condo made it obvious that the unit needed renovation to re-rent it. And those renovations would lose value with the wear and tear of the next tenant. So, what to do?

A search of the sales in the community showed us that units there were going for up to a maximum sale price of $92,000. That was a $12,000 increase in average price in just one year! But what if we made it even better than those? Could we ask even higher? Could we keep expenses to a minimum and turn a decent profit after materials, labor, commissions, and closing fees? I definitely thought we could, and with Covid closures, and being out of school, Eric had the time to participate in doing the work and learn about renovating at the same time.

It's interesting when you tell a story like this—in hindsight. I mean, it all sounds so simple when told in just a few paragraphs. When you look in the rearview mirror, it sounds so smooth: we had a unit, the tenant left, we renovated it, and sold it. Success! But in reality, that's not how it felt at the time. If you put yourself into the moment, everything was uncertain at the time. It felt so unsettling to wonder if the economy was going to go into a tailspin, if we would find a buyer before the association dues ate into all of the savings, and if we'd be able to sell the property at the right price to make it worthwhile.

Being in the moment can cause one to feel that way—unsure and scared. That's why I wanted to include this part about the unexpected. When the unexpected does happen, and it often does, we can all have a tendency to think the worst. Please try to avoid that. The beauty of investing is that when you own the asset, you control everything.

Some calm reflection showed that we did indeed have options. We could:

Re-rent the property-- (although it would take some reno) Refinance the property—the property had gone up in value and we could have explored refinancing it with a bank and pulling cash out and then leasing it again. There is actually an investment strategy where people do this. They buy a property in cash, fix it, and then pull the cash out with financing. It's called the BRRR method (buy, renovate, rent, refinance) and it's a very valid investment strategy.
Sell the property—this was our choice. Since Eric was out of school anyways, and we were still social distancing, this was something that we could take on as a DIY project, keep ourselves busy at the condo, and learn about renovating firsthand.

The decision to renovate the condo wasn't just about salvaging the investment—it was about teaching Eric the value of hard work, perseverance, and the ability to pivot when faced with challenges. We rolled up our sleeves and got to work, turning the vacant condo into a family project.

The renovation journey began…

Lesson 11: Property Renovation. Enhancing Value with DIY Projects

During the renovation, we focused on projects that would provide the highest return on investment. The great thing about working with a condo is that you limit your scope of repairs to the interior of the unit. After all, the roof, exterior of the building, and the landscaping were all covered by the condo association. This is very convenient when undertaking your first flip, because you limit the potential for unknown expenses.

If you've ever been inside a property during a rainstorm and heard the sudden, shocking, steady drip, drip, drip of raindrops coming through a leak in the roof and hitting the floor, and been gripped by the fear of what that unexpected expense might cost, you'll know why its nice to avoid worrying about exterior repairs on a first flip project.

Inside, we tackled cost-effective renovations that significantly boosted the condo's value. These included updating the kitchen and appliances, refreshing the bathroom, and installing modern fixtures throughout the home. Each project was chosen to maximize the property's appeal to potential buyers while keeping costs in check.

Tried and True

When flipping properties in the US, there are certain upgrades that consistently offer the best return on investment (ROI). Here are a few of the most popular and most effective ones:

Kitchen Remodel:

A minor kitchen remodel typically yields one of the highest ROIs. I know it sounds expensive, but updating countertops, cabinets, and appliances can significantly increase a property's value, and they don't always have to cost a fortune. Even small changes, like replacing hardware or adding a fresh coat of paint, can make a big difference. Some older cabinets don't have any hardware at all, and you can buy some very modern pulls, add them to the cabinet fronts, and quickly modernize a kitchen. Fixtures are another great place to upgrade. A new modern kitchen faucet doesn't cost too much and can upgrade the look of the kitchen right away. I've been showing homes for over 20 years, and the kitchen is consistently the first place buyers gravitate to when looking at the home. It's often the first room they head to because if the kitchen is great, then they feel better about the rest of the home.

Bathroom Renovation:

Upgrading bathrooms with paint, new tiles, or modern vanities, tends to provide a strong return. Even minor improvements, like re-caulking the tub or updating the lighting, can make the space feel cleaner and more appealing. You'd be surprised at how changing shower fixtures can update a bathroom, and the cost is truly minimal--and you can do it yourself.

Curb Appeal:

First impressions matter, and curb appeal is critical. Investing in landscaping, exterior painting, and improving the entryway (e.g., a new front door or upgraded lighting) can significantly boost a property's marketability and value. Projects like adding a new garage door or improving the driveway also offer good returns. These items didn't matter for us in the condo, but, it's important to note that curb appeal remains one of the top go-to areas for significant improvement. I always tell sellers to make sure their doorway is very clean and inviting. It will always take the Realtor a few moments to get the key out of the lockbox and get the door open, and buyers always look up and around during that little period of time. Providing them with a view of a clean porch or pretty flowers and an inviting rug sets the tone for their visit of the home.

Energy-Efficient Upgrades:

Installing energy-efficient windows, doors, and insulation not only appeals to environmentally conscious buyers but also reduces utility costs, making the property more attractive. These upgrades can often be marketed as cost-saving features. In my state of Florida, for example, electricity costs are sometimes exorbitant. Especially with homes that have older windows. Newer homes have energy efficient windows, and sometimes even spray foam insulation in the concrete block, to help lower the energy costs. So, having new windows is a significant improvement that many buyers will appreciate. Solar panels are also good improvements if they're something that you wanted for yourself--but I wouldn't recommend adding them specifically for a sale. Many solar panels come with a monthly charge for the equipment that some buyers don't want to take on, so I'd say this is more of a location specific upgrade.

Flooring:

Replacing old carpet or worn-out flooring with hardwood or high-quality flooring can dramatically increase a home's appeal. Hardwood floors, in particular, are highly sought after by buyers and can justify a higher asking price, but they are expensive, so you'll need to balance that with your budget. We have used water-resistant luxury vinyl plank many times and it has been cost effective and an easy DIY project, and it looks great.

Open Floor Plan:

You see it on all of the renovation shows on TV, right? The beautiful couple who are renovating a home-- they kick down a wall and suddenly the whole home opens up into a beautiful palatial space. It's true, modern buyers often prefer open, spacious layouts, and removing non-load-bearing walls to create a more open floor plan can make a home feel larger and more inviting, which can lead to a higher selling price. However, this isn't always possible (or safe) when you're taking on a renovation yourself. So, approach this one with caution. Try to work with what you have and see if there are alternative solutions to removing entire walls.

We got to work on our condo flip, focusing on low cost but high impact upgrades. As Eric can now attest to, it takes a <u>long</u> time to find the right products that look expensive and are great quality, but while remaining very budget friendly.

I sometimes take hours finding the right products. I will provide a link to my go-to favorites, and a link to the downloadable budget worksheet on my website under the resources section.
https://marciasocas.com/**building-wealth-resources/**

Sample Project Budget Worksheet

Kitchen	Amount needed	Cost		General	Amount needed	Cost
Kitchen				**General**		
Cabinets				Interior Paint		
Cabinet Pulls				Flooring		
Countertops				Baseboards		
Backsplash				Windows		
Sink				Doors		
Faucet				Lights		
Garbage Disposal				Fans		
Refrigerator				Blinds/shades		
Dishwasher				Closet shelving		
Stove						
Oven				**Major upgrades**		
Microwave				HVAC		
Flooring				Plumbing		
Lighting				Electrical		
				Roof		

Bathroom	Amount needed	Cost		Exterior	Amount needed	Cost
Bathroom				**Exterior**		
Vanity				Seal and Paint		
Countertop				Landscaping		
Faucet				Pool repairs		
Shower Fixtures				Fence		
Tile						
Flooring						
Wallpaper						
Paint						
Lighting						
Tub						
Toilet						

The Condo Flip

While I don't want to go into too many specific details regarding the repairs we made, since your property flip may need different upgrades, I did want to go through a few of the upgrades in order to share how we overcame some common problems.

The Kitchen

The kitchen cabinets were a dingy old yellowy beige, the Formica laminate counters were in good condition but really dated, and the appliances worked but were not ideal for selling. Since this is a small kitchen, it's really worth the money when doing a condo flip to get some great granite and stainless-steel appliances in here so that a buyer will fall in love with it.

In order to save money in the condo flip, and because the cabinets were really in good condition on the inside, we removed the doors and kept and painted the cabinet boxes. We used a Cabinet Transformation kit which comes with paint that goes on wonderfully and doesn't leave drips. *Please note, if you're going to paint cabinets it's always important to start with only a very light first coat for a smooth application.*

We only painted the cabinet boxes. In order to get the most professional finish possible, we purchased new cabinet doors. Since cabinets come in standard sizes, replacing the doors was easy and quick. We saved money and time by not replacing the entire cabinetry. The large hardware stores sell the replacement doors, so they're not difficult to find at all. We also purchased nice cabinet pulls to make the kitchen look much more modern.

We also decided to remove the kitchen floor tile. With new flooring going into the main living room, and the kitchen area being relatively small, it just made sense to use Eric's free labor to get that tile broken up and out of there.

I think he had fun with the sledgehammer. After all, he's still young and being allowed to break something is kind of fun.

We also changed the countertops. If you can go to a granite yard you can often find a leftover slab that was part of a larger lot. I've had success in buying these single slabs at a discount and having a granite installer cut them to size. It has been much more cost effective than it may sound on the surface. By the way, one of the great things when changing out the granite is that you can change the area of the countertops. We felt like the original counters were a little too small. We worked with the granite fabricator to cut the granite a bit more generously at the corner.

The other great thing about changing the counters in this condo flip is that you get to install updated new fixtures, like a sink and faucet. Updating the sink and faucet change the look immediately.

The Bathroom

A new vanity was definitely needed, for the condo flip and Eric picked it up from the hardware store. We kept it easy by buying one that came with the top already. We also replaced the lighting. This is always a good idea because lighting is such an easy and inexpensive way to update a space.

The Bedroom and Other Areas

We immediately painted the walls throughout the unit with a neutral color, which, when combined with crisp white doors and baseboards, makes every property look great.

As for the flooring, we removed the old carpet and replaced it with luxury vinyl plank. I don't know if you've seen this flooring yet, but it's extremely easy to install and looks great. It utilizes a click and lock system, and it's inexpensive. Unlike the old laminate flooring system which chipped or suffered when it was wet, the luxury vinyl plank is water resistant and scratch resistant as well. It's cost effective and easy.

So easy an 18-year-old working on his first flip can do it!

The process wasn't always smooth, but it was incredibly rewarding. Eric saw firsthand how much effort goes into improving a property, and he learned that the value of an asset isn't just in its market price, but also in the care and work you invest in it. By the time the renovation was complete, the condo had transformed from a simple rental property into a valuable asset ready for sale.

The Sale!!

We were so happy with the results of this condo flip! The highest sale price in the neighborhood was $92,000, but we felt that our unit was updated more than most, so we pushed it and went for a price of $105,000. Luckily for us, the very first person who viewed it placed a full price offer.

When it came time for the appraisal, we left a sheet on the kitchen counter. In it we showed sales in the neighboring area that would support our price. We also left a list of all of the upgrades to the property. This prompted the appraiser to take those into consideration.

The property appraised and we sold the unit for $105,000. This was the highest price in the community for a 1 bedroom unit in over 12 years! (since the market highs back then).

Our process in this condo flip took 3 weeks for the condo renovation. We were on the market for only a day or two before receiving the full price contract. The buyer was obtaining financing, so that process took 30 days to get to closing.

When it came time for closing, we were excited, but then it was delayed. This is the way things sometimes go, so be ready for it. Changes to lending delayed the financing. It was tense for a while, but remember that when you have the property, you have the asset, and although it may take longer, you will sell. In our case it took 2 weeks longer than expected, but sure enough closing day came along, Eric paid back the mortgage (with interest) and came away from the experience with $26,911.27 in profit!

I hope this shows you that you shouldn't be afraid to take on a renovation or embark on your first flip.

Lesson 12: Budgeting and Working with Contractors

Working with Contractors:

You may decide to work with a contractor rather than doing the renovation yourself on your fix and flip project. I often use a handyman, one that I work with very regularly, on my renovation projects. Finding him took a long time, there were lots of handymen along the way that let me down, but now having him on a renovation project is worth his weight in gold.

If you are working with someone, whether it's a handyman or contractor, here are some suggestions to help you along that process.

1. Do Your Homework

Before you even think about hiring someone, do your research. Look for contractors with a solid track record and good reviews. I often see handymen and/or contractors being spoken about on local apps like the Nextdoor app. Alternatively, you can simply speak with neighbors in your community. Ask friends or family for recommendations, and be sure to check online reviews. Trust me, a little digging now can save you headaches later.

2. Get Multiple Bids

It's tempting to go with the first contractor who gives you a reasonable price quote, but take your time. Get at least three bids so you can compare what each contractor is offering and how long the job will take them. It's also nice to see what different professionals recommend. You may get an idea that could save you some time and money.

3. Verify Licenses and Insurance

If you're working with a contractor, ask for verification of their license and insurance. You don't want someone working on your property if they don't have their own insurance in case of any mishaps.

4. Communicate Clearly

Clear communication is the key to any successful project. Set up regular check-ins, and don't hesitate to voice your expectations. Document everything—timelines, budgets, the scope of work—so there's no room for misunderstandings. I have a resource that you can use on my website. Just download it and it'll help you budget and plan the timeline clearly, so that you can have things planned out in writing.

5. Have a Solid Contract

Your contract with the contractor should spell out all the details, from the materials being used to the payment schedule. You'll need to decide if you're getting the materials, or if the contractor is. (I always get the materials for our projects. This allows me to make sure that no one else is marking up pricing, allows me to negotiate where possible, and provides me with reward points when purchasing from the big box hardware stores.) A well-drafted contract protects everyone involved and ensures that the project stays on track.

6. Set Up a Payment Plan

Instead of paying everything upfront, break the payments into milestones. *Never pay for a job in full upfront.* This way, you're only paying for work that's been completed to your satisfaction. It's a fair system for both you and the contractor.

7. Be Flexible but Firm, and Expect the Unexpected

Renovations rarely go exactly as planned, so be prepared to adapt. That being said, stay firm on your budget and quality expectations, as well as the timeline. No matter how well you plan, surprises are inevitable. Set aside a contingency fund—10-20% of your budget is a good rule of thumb—to cover any unexpected costs. This will keep the project moving smoothly, even when things don't go exactly as planned.

8. Build a Relationship

A good relationship with your contractor (or handyman) can make all the difference. Treat them with respect, stay responsive, and show genuine appreciation for a job well done. A positive working relationship can lead to smoother projects and even better deals down the line.

9. Be Part of the Process

Don't wait until the project is done to check the work. Regular inspections let you catch any issues early on, so they can be fixed before they turn into bigger problems. Visit the work site, it'll show that this project is important to you, and it will make it important to others.

How You Can Do This Yourself: The Power of Sweat Equity

- **Renovate**: Renovating a property yourself, or with the help of family, can significantly increase your return on investment. Sweat equity—putting in the work yourself—reduces costs and gives you control over the quality of the work. Being willing to get involved in renovations, from painting to installing fixtures, not only saves money but also allows you to customize the property to suit the market.
- **Choose your first project carefully:** When taking on your first property, consider starting with one that has limited exposure to risk. For example, by starting with a condo, you can really just focus on the inside of the property and limit your need for help (and expense) on larger, structural, exterior projects.

Legacy: How you can help your children or grandchildren start

- **Working together:** One of the most rewarding aspects of this project was the bonding experience it provided. It can be surprising to learn how little young people know today about construction and household projects. We've learned these things over time, and getting involved together physically on projects passes on valuable knowledge and allows for some great times together.

- **Provide a down payment as a gift:** As parents or grandparents, you can support young adults by providing a down payment as a graduation gift, but the value extends far beyond the financial investment. Involving them in the planning and execution of the project teaches valuable life skills and motivates them to take ownership of their financial future. Watching Eric take the lead on the renovation, seeing his confidence grow, and witnessing the final successful flip was incredibly fulfilling.

- **If financially feasible for you, make the loan:** This chapter wouldn't be complete without discussing the role of family support in a young investor's journey. Whether it's parents or grandparents, family can play a critical role in providing financial backing, such as offering a mortgage for young investors. I shared how we structured Eric's mortgage, making sure he understood the responsibility that came with it. This wasn't just a loan—it was a stepping stone toward financial independence.

- **Cosign on the loan:** If your child or grandchild has limited credit history, or if co-signing on a mortgage can help them qualify for better terms and get their foot in the door of real estate investing.

Chapter 4
College

Nailing Down Success.
From College Housing to Airbnb
Cash Flow Machine

Chapter Four: Nailing Down Success.
From College Housing to Airbnb Cash Flow Machine

Again, time passed, the University opened again after having been closed due to the pandemic. Soon, Eric was finishing his 2nd year. He had lived with several roommates in an apartment that year and was now looking forward to living on his own for the upcoming year. He still had 3 years of schooling left, because he was part of an accelerated 5-year program that allowed students to obtain both their undergraduate degree and their MBA within a 5-year span. Knowing that he had 3 full years left, it only made sense to try to once again look for real estate and see if it was more cost effective to buy than to rent again.

We drove up to Tuscaloosa at the beginning of the summer, ready to start the search. I had my heart set on a cute, small condo close to the school. Something that didn't have high condo dues and that felt safe. I had researched some properties online and we met with a Realtor up there who took us to see a few places. As we were in her car, we started chitchatting a bit, just something to get to know each other and avoid awkward silence in the car.

She started, "So, how do you folks like the University of Alabama? It's such a big campus—I imagine there's always something going on for Eric."

"Oh, yes, he seems to love it." I answered, "I love how beautiful the campus is, and Eric seems really happy here. Since he still has 3 years left, it makes sense for us to consider buying a property here, it seems like it would potentially cost less than renting and wasting that money. Plus," I said, jokingly, "if he has a place here maybe we can come up for a football game."

At this point my husband John chimed in, "Well, who knows if we could even get tickets at this point. With them being National Champs, I don't know how tough tickets would be."

She answered him, "You might be able to find tickets online, but finding a place to stay is really the tough part! Bryant-Denny Stadium holds over 100,000 fans. On game days, the whole town practically shuts down. It gets so crowded; you wouldn't believe it. But there are only about 5,000 hotel rooms in Tuscaloosa itself, so you can imagine how quickly they fill up."

"Wow, only 5,000 rooms? I can see why they're building those expensive new million-dollar condos by the stadium; I assume those are for wealthy alumni, or corporate owners, who want to go to the games."

"Exactly! A lot of visitors end up staying in Birmingham, but that's almost an hour away. It's another reason why short-term rentals in Tuscaloosa can do so well. There's tons of demand during football season, graduation, and other events."

At that point, we arrived at the first condo and looked around. I loved the condos, and the pricing seemed reasonable. Eric, however, wasn't quite as happy about them and told me that there were a few areas we had visited that were known for recent car break-ins.

"Well, we'll have to think about these a little bit and decide what to do then." I thanked the Realtor for her time and we went back to the hotel to think about our next steps.

I'll be honest, I was a little frustrated at this point. I felt that I knew what was best, and that it was going to be an inexpensive one-bedroom condo and that would be that. I was ready to sign on one of those today. But Eric wasn't. I realized that I had to allow Eric to take charge of this process a little, and I had to trust that the real estate lessons to date had taken root. We would see what tomorrow would bring…

Lesson 13: Finding the Deal, Thinking Creatively, and How to Calculate ROI

The next day, we sat down to a hearty southern style breakfast together, ready to discuss options once again. I felt that if we couldn't decide on a one-bedroom condo, then maybe we needed to discuss renting again.

Eric seemed prepared with some thoughts. He started, "Mom, I've been thinking about it."

"OK, I said, did you decide that any of the ones we saw yesterday would work?"

"No," he continued. "I've been thinking that I don't want a condo. I really want a house."

A house?

I hadn't thought about a house. That was a different price point and also came with responsibilities like cutting the grass and maintaining the exterior. I just hadn't thought about it as an option.

"But Eric," I objected, "a house has a lot more maintenance, and it's not like we can find a one-bedroom house. And they cost more. So, let's say we find a three-bedroom house. You'll have roommates again, and you said you didn't want that."

"No, no," he said, "I definitely don't want roommates."

No roommates. A house. And no roommates to pay rent.

He was piercing his breakfast potatoes, amusedly stacking them up on the fork, as if what he had just told me was the most normal thing in the world.

I felt myself getting hot. Where was this entitlement coming from? How could he possibly think he could have a house, and no roommates? This went against every financially responsible lesson I felt that he'd had growing up.

I think he must have seen the seething and shocked looked on my face and he quickly spoke to clarify things.

"Wait, mom, hear me out. I have a plan I want to run by you."

After that, he proceeded to tell me about his plan, and about how he'd stayed up looking at short-term rental rates in the area. The conversation with the Realtor in the car had stayed with him, and he saw the lack of hotel rooms as a need to be filled in the area.

"I know there are some Airbnbs throughout Tuscaloosa, and I know there's a chance the Realtor underestimated the number of hotel rooms; but let's just bring up the number and say there are 7000 places to say. And each of those holds an average of 4 people. Some Airbnbs may hold more but some hotel rooms may hold only 2. So if we average 4, or even 5 people per room, that puts us at lodging for 35,000 people. There are around 35,000 students as well. So that's a total of 70,000 people with a place to stay. That still leaves 30,000 that might like to stay in Tuscaloosa for a big game day weekend but can't because there's no room."

OK, I thought, I do see the need for short-term rental housing on big weekends. But you can't have roommates that would leave a house for a weekend.

"Exactly," he said. "I don't want roommates. I don't want to keep living in a situation where I have roommates who can invite over people that I don't like or that get belligerent in our place. And I don't want to have to deal with people having a party when I need to study. This way I can avoid roommates. I could probably charge a roommate $600 per month. But I researched the going rate on Airbnb and VRBO, and some of those big game weekends go for at least $1500 per night. There are 7 home games this season, that's 14 nights, Fridays and Saturdays. Obviously, they won't all go for $1500 per night, but even if only two of those are 'big weekends', and the rest are kind of average, I'd be making at least $6000 for the two big weekends, and then let's say just $600 per night average on the other ones. Those smaller weekends would be $600 x 10. That means $6000 total for the smaller weekends, and $6000 total for the two big ones. That's $12,000 in a year. That's the same as I'd get from 2 roommates. And that's not even counting basketball season or graduation, and graduation is huge."

My head was spinning with all of the numbers he was throwing at me. But, even more, my heart was swelling with joy at the fact that he had assessed a situation and found a problem that needed a solution and found a way to do that with an asset. He really had internalized the lessons and the way of thinking that I had tried to pass on to him, and I was so very proud.

That afternoon we looked at some homes and started to open our minds to the possibility of owning an Airbnb in a college town. We would purchase it under the name of the LLC that Eric had started back at his 8th grade graduation. The company would pay him a salary for managing the property during the year. On big weekends, he would leave the house, locking his room, and stay with a friend for the weekend.

Additionally, since we were going to have the house as an Airbnb, I wondered if we might be able to write off some expenses that we normally would be paying for with "after tax" dollars. For example, electricity, cable, lawncare, water, gas, and internet. This made it even more attractive!

Please note that according to the IRS.gov website as of the date of this writing,

If you rent a dwelling unit to others that you also use as a residence, limitations may apply to the rental expenses you can deduct. You're considered to use a dwelling unit as a residence if you use it for personal purposes during the tax year for a number of days that's more than the greater of:

1. *14 days, or*

2. *10% of the total days you rent it to others at a fair rental price.*

So, Eric living there would be considered personal use, <u>unless he was charged fair market rent.</u> Be sure to follow the proper rules and regulations, you can find them on the irs.gov website.

Since Eric was going to have the benefit of living in the property, and the asset would be generating income that would pay for the mortgage, and we'd be able to sell that asset when he graduated, the purchase of the house became a logical choice. While our calculations included just some rough numbers, since there were clearly so many advantages to the purchase for us, you may want to run your numbers a little more carefully if you're investing in a property to use as a short-term rental.

Here's a look at how you'd do that:

Analyzing ROI

Analyzing the potential return on investment (ROI) for a short-term rental property involves several key steps. Here are some step-by-step guidelines for you to use.

1. Estimate Potential Income

- **Average Nightly Rate**: Research similar properties in the area to determine the average nightly rate. You can use platforms like Airbnb, and Vrbo, to get this information. Select sample dates and check out pricing at different times throughout the year.

- **Occupancy Rate**: Calculate the expected occupancy rate. The occupancy rate is the percentage of days in a year that you expect the property to be rented. For example, a 70% occupancy rate means you expect the property to be rented for about 256 nights a year. You can again use platforms like Airbnb, and Vrbo, to get this information. You can use the map feature to zoom into the same area you're researching. Then select some properties that are similar, and scroll down and take a look at their calendar. You'll be able to see how many dates are already booked up. This will give you an idea of the occupancy for a particular time of year, or even special weekends (like graduation weekend and football weekends in our case).

- **Gross Rental Income**: Multiply the average nightly rate by the expected number of rented nights (Occupancy Rate x 365 days). This gives you the estimated gross rental income for the year. Your analysis may be a little more detailed if you're counting on different rates during different high and low seasons, but the generalization is the same—you're looking to calculate what you think your rental income for the year could be.

Formula:

Gross Rental Income= Average Nightly Rate × Occupancy Rate × 365

2. Calculate Operating Expenses

- **Property Management Fees**: If you plan to use a property management company, this typically costs 10-30% of your rental income. By the way, I've generally found that property management fees can be quite negotiable, so don't be afraid to ask.

- **Cleaning Fees**: Estimate the cost of cleaning the property between guest stays. This can either be charged to guests or absorbed as an expense. I typically add it into the guest fees in the short-term rental listing. Also, keep your communication with your cleaners close. Be sure to have their cell so that they can ask you questions right away if they need you, and they can send you photos of any issues or sent you pictures of the cleaned property prior to guest arrival. Eric always performed a "pre guest arrival" video so that he would have a record of the condition that the home was left in, in case there were any complaints or damages. Luckily, we never had an issue, but the walk through video was there 'just in case' and it only took a minute to do.

- **Utilities**: Include costs for electricity, water, gas, internet, cable, etc. These will be just an estimate at first but when buying a property you can ask the seller what their average fees were for these items so that you can use those in your budget.

- **Maintenance and Repairs**: Set aside a budget for regular maintenance and repairs.

- **Insurance**: Include the cost of homeowners insurance and additional liability insurance for short-term rentals. Note that some platforms, like Airbnb currently, provide insurance coverage built into their program. So, be sure to read what each platform offers you so that you aren't paying for something that's already included as a benefit to you.

- **Property Taxes**: Don't forget to include local property taxes.

- **Supplies**: Costs for restocking essentials like toiletries, linens, etc.

- **Marketing and Listing Fees**: Include any costs associated with listing the property on rental platforms, such as Airbnb service fees.

Formula:

Operating Expenses=Sum of all monthly expenses×12

3. Calculate Net Operating Income (NOI)

- **Net Operating Income (NOI)**: Subtract the total operating expenses from the gross rental income.

Formula:

NOI=Gross Rental Income−Operating Expenses

4. Estimate Capital Expenditures (CapEx)

- These are funds used to improve the property and extend its life, such as roof replacements or major renovations. While not an annual expense, it's good to budget for it over time.

Example:
Set aside 5-10% of your NOI for CapEx.

5. Calculate Cash Flow

- **Cash Flow**: Subtract any mortgage payments or loan servicing costs from your NOI. This gives you the cash flow, which is the amount of money you'll have left over each month or year after all expenses are paid.

Formula:

Cash Flow=NOI−Mortgage Payments

6. Calculate ROI

- **Initial Investment**: Add up all initial costs, including the down payment, closing costs, and any immediate renovation or furnishing expenses.

- **Annual Cash Flow**: Multiply your monthly cash flow by 12 to get your annual cash flow.

- **ROI Calculation**: Divide the annual cash flow by your initial investment to get the ROI percentage.

Formula:

$$ROI = (\text{Annual Cash Flow/Initial Investment}) \times 100$$

7. Consider Appreciation and Tax Benefits

- **Property Appreciation**: Factor in the expected appreciation of the property value over time.

- **Tax Benefits**: Consider any tax deductions, such as depreciation, mortgage interest, and other property-related expenses, which can improve your overall ROI.

Example:

Let's say you're considering a property with the following details:

- **Purchase Price**: $300,000
- **Down Payment**: $60,000
- **Average Nightly Rate**: $160
- **Occupancy Rate**: 70%
- **Annual Operating Expenses**: $25,000
- **Mortgage Payments**: $1,200/month

Steps:

1. **Gross Rental Income**:
   $160/night x 256 nights = $40,960/year

2. **Operating Expenses**:
   $20,000/year

3. **NOI**:
   $40,960 - $20,000 = $20,960/year

4. **Cash Flow**:
   $20,960 - ($1,200 x 12) = $20,960 - $14,400 = $6,560

5. **ROI**:
   If the property appreciates and you gain tax benefits, the ROI could be higher than the initial cash flow suggests. But based purely on cash flow:
   ROI = $6560 / $60,000 = 10.93%

This analysis gives you a snapshot of the financial viability of a short-term rental property, helping you make informed investment decisions.

So, in this straightforward example, your $60,000 is giving you a return of almost 11% per year, plus your $600,000 investment is presumably growing in value (as real estate typically does) as well. Additionally, you're benefiting from depreciation on your tax returns. And, in our case, we would have spent the money on the operating expense for Eric to live at college *anyways*—this provided a way for the company, and Airbnb income, to pay for those expenses.

I've set up an interactive spreadsheet to help you calculate your own potential ROI on a property. It's free for download and available at: https://marciasocas.com/**building-wealth-resources/**

Lesson 14: Setting up a Short-Term Rental Property

The house Eric loved was a 3-bedroom, 2-bath home with a large living room, and large fenced-in backyard. It was located just 2 miles from the football stadium, and had a long driveway, making it comfortable for several cars without anyone parking in the street.

Now that we were set on buying the house, we needed to make sure we could use it as a short-term rental.

Local laws and licensing

If you're purchasing a property for use as a short-term rental, you'll need to ensure that it is zoned for short-term rental use. I recommend adding a clause into your purchase contract stating that your contract is contingent on short-term rental use, and that the seller will assist in any applications for the zoning. This way, you'll have the property under contract, and have the time to make sure that you have the necessary approval from any local zoning authority or state licensure.

In our case, the home that we decided on was located in an area that was not automatically zoned for short-term rental. However, there was a process in place to request a variance in the zoning. We filled out the application right away and submitted it to the zoning. In our particular case, the home required variance approval, as well as a short-term rental application. As part of the process, we had to show that a home inspection was performed confirming that the property was up to standards. We also needed to provide evidence of adequate insurance, and we obtained a business license with the city of Tuscaloosa.

Checklist for Local Laws and Licensure

1. **Research Zoning Laws**

   - Verify if short-term rentals are allowed in the property's zoning district.

   - Check for any restrictions or special requirements for operating a short-term rental in residential areas.

2. **Obtain Required Permits**

   - Determine if a short-term rental permit is required by the city, county, or state.

   - Understand the application process, including any fees, inspections, or documentation needed.

   - Confirm if a special use permit is necessary for certain types of properties or locations.

3. **Licensing Requirements**

   - Find out if you need a business license to operate a short-term rental.

   - Check if the property must be licensed as a lodging establishment or similar classification.

   - Investigate whether you need to renew licenses annually or periodically.

4. **Understand Occupancy Limits**

   - Review local regulations regarding the maximum number of guests allowed per property or per room.

   - Ensure compliance with fire safety and building codes that may dictate occupancy limits.

5. **Compliance with Health and Safety Standards**

   - Confirm that the property meets local health and safety standards, including fire alarms, carbon monoxide detectors, and emergency exits.

- Schedule any required health or safety inspections prior to operating the rental.

6. **Short-Term Rental Tax Obligations**

   - Determine if you need to collect and remit occupancy taxes, also known as transient occupancy taxes (TOT) or lodging taxes.

   - Register with local tax authorities if required, and understand the filing process and deadlines.

   - Investigate any additional taxes, such as sales tax or gross receipts tax, that may apply.

7. **Restrictions on Length of Stay**

   - Check for minimum or maximum stay requirements, such as prohibitions on stays shorter than a certain number of nights. I currently own a short-term rental condo in St Petersburg and the rules are different there. Over there, you can rent your property out for less than 30 days only 3 times per year; but you can rent it for stays of 31 days or greater as often as you'd like. Therefore, sometimes I'll have someone who wants to stay for 4 weeks (28 days), and since I don't want their stay to count as a strike against me in the "under 30 days" limitation, I typically will offer this traveler an additional three days free. They're happy because of the free nights, I'm happy because I don't use up one of my shorter stay options which I can use for a busier and more expensive time (like the 4th of July week). It's important to know the rules so that you can follow and utilize them properly.

   - Be aware of any limitations on how many days per year the property can be rented out as a short-term rental. *You'll see that this item affected us with the college home project.*

8. **Insurance Requirements**

- Verify if additional liability insurance is required for short-term rentals. Remember to look at what is already included with various online platforms for owners, as some short-term rental platforms do already offer owners some built-in coverage for issues.

- Determine whether standard homeowners' insurance will cover short-term rental activities or if you need a specialized policy.

9. **Signage and Advertising Regulations**

- Review local laws regarding signage, such as prohibitions on advertising the property as a short-term rental on-site.

- Understand any rules related to online advertising, including required disclosures on platforms like Airbnb or Vrbo.

10. **Homeowners Association (HOA) Rules**

- If the property is within an HOA, review the HOA's rules and regulations related to short-term rentals.

- Obtain written approval from the HOA if required and understand any additional fees or restrictions imposed by the association. The short-term rental condo that I have in St Petersburg, for example, requires a $100 fee for every rental.

11. **Noise and Nuisance Ordinances**

- Familiarize yourself with local noise ordinances and quiet hours that could affect your guests.

- Understand your responsibilities as a property owner in preventing nuisances, such as excessive noise or parking issues.

12. Rental Agreements and Contracts

- Draft rental agreements that comply with local laws, including mandatory disclosures and house rules.

- Include clauses that address compliance with local laws and penalties for violations.

When it came time for our zoning application, Eric appeared before the zoning board via an online video call. They asked him to confirm the number of occupants he was requesting approval for, as well as the number of cars. They asked him to ensure that the rules of the house would state that there were no loud parties allowed and asked him about potential noise issues with neighbors. After some discussion, they approved the house for the zoning variance and the short-term rental!

And yet, once again, something unexpected happened.

I'd had a short-term rental condo close to Disney World in the past, and rented it on a consistent basis. I had it advertised 365 days a year. So, when the approval from the city of Tuscaloosa came, I was a bit taken aback. The approval for properties allowed as short-term rentals was done on a probationary basis for the first year. That meant that the total number of nights that the home could be rented out was 30 nights in the entire calendar year. We had to ensure that we could make the money we needed to cover the mortgage (and equate to what full time roommates would theoretically pay) with only 30 nights of rental. And Eric would have to ensure that the home would be approved for renewal the following year, since this was just a probationary period.

We ran our calculations again and were happy with the numbers we could expect from the year's football schedule, along with the graduation weekend. Eric went and spoke with his neighbors, introducing himself and making sure they had his cell phone number in case anyone caused any noise disturbance at any time at all. He explained that he was going to rent out the house to offset his housing expenses while in college, and they seemed happy with him and his determination as a young real estate investor and entrepreneur.

Now, it was time to prepare the home to maximize income.

Renovations and Furnishings:

When setting up a short-term rental, it is important to create an inviting space with modern amenities and comfortable furnishings.

When setting one up in an area where you hope to charge more than others, and ensure maximum occupancy, you need to be a bit "extra."

After all, if you're heading into your old college town, ready to spend a significant amount of money to get together with some friends, would you choose the home with plain drab furnishings or one that comes alive with the colors of your alma matter, with your favorite team mascot on display, and homage paid to the great features of your school?

Similarly, if you're off to a beach vacation and decide to rent a place, would you be quicker to select the one with motel like finishes or one that pops with coastal blues and whites, with shiplap and wood accents, and beach décor to add to the vacation feeling?

Although specific numerical data regarding pricing and occupancy rates may not be easily accessible, these factors are well-recognized in the short-term rental industry as contributing to increased desirability and potentially higher income.

1. **Market Differentiation**: Properties that stand out due to unique themes or decor are more likely to attract attention from potential renters browsing through listings. This differentiation can lead to higher occupancy rates as guests are often willing to pay a premium for a memorable experience.

2. **Guest Experience**: Themed rooms create a more immersive and enjoyable stay, which can result in better reviews. Positive reviews are crucial for improving your property's visibility on platforms like Airbnb and can justify higher nightly rates.

3. **Higher Rental Income**: Unique decor, especially themed rooms that appeal to specific demographics (such as families with children, fans of certain movies or sports), can justify higher rental prices. Guests are often willing to pay more for a stay that offers something out of the ordinary.

When it came time to setting up the college game day home, we set up the two available bedrooms, each with it's own theme. One bedroom was based on Bear Bryant, the legendary football coach. Bear was known for wearing his black and white houndstooth hat and so we brought this theme into the room. We hung a large, framed photo of Bear on one wall, and printed out and framed several of his famously inspiring quotes to hang along another wall. We took advantage of a coat rack the prior owner had left behind and decorated it with a houndstooth hat and scarf. For the nightstands, we purchased some that looked like football lockers, and along the back wall we added a section of chalkboard paint and drew out football plays with their characteristic x's and o's. We left the chalk there for guests to add their own plays or notes, and we could just erase them when they left. Those touches, paired with simple black sheets, a white comforter, and decorative pillows were all that were needed to instantly create a theme. The only real expense was the Bear Bryant wall hanging, everything else was just color choices and some minor decorative touches. But the effect was fantastic, and guests loved the room.

In the second room, we created a theme based on the year that the school was founded, 1831. We went to the local office supply store and printed out photos of the university when it opened, along with a print of the school logo and a printed explanation of the elements in the logo. We placed those in large inexpensive frames on the wall. The nightstands were kept rustic to go with the theme, and the few decorative elements were ones that looked somewhat antique. We utilized the school colors in this room, through their use in the bedlinens and comforter.

The large showstopper was a mural at the entryway. The school mascot is an elephant known as "Big Al." I found a large elephant mural, which was just a peel and stick wallpaper, online and suddenly we had a larger-than-life elephant seemingly charging through the wall.

What I've noticed about short-term rentals is that you can be much bolder with décor than you ever would be in your own home. People like to allow themselves to be immersed in a feeling or a theme when they're on vacation, so play into that and stand out with your décor. It will make your place memorable and help with your reviews.

Essential Amenities

While discussing finishes for your short-term rental, we should also address the essential items that your guests will want to see when they arrive.

After all, can you imagine checking into your stay, running to use the bathroom after a long car ride and lots of snacks and drinks, and not having toilet paper?

These are the fundamental items that guests expect for a comfortable stay, and a few that make your location stand out.

Basic linens to have on hand

Bedding, along with an extra set in the closet.
2 Extra pillows to keep in the closet of each bedroom.
Towels—I aim for 2 towels per guest
Washcloths—I prefer dark grey or black because that way small discolorations from makeup won't show. I used to use white, but I had to constantly buy more.

Bathroom Amenities

Providing hotel-like amenities enhances comfort and convenience.

Hair Dryer
Extra Toothbrushes and Toothpaste
Cotton Swabs and Cotton Balls
Tissues
Non-Slip Shower Mat
Plunger and Toilet Brush – having a plunger on hand will prevent some maintenance calls to you, so don't skimp out on this one
Laundry Hamper or Bag (optional)
Soap (hand soap and shower soap or shower gel)
Shampoo and conditioner
Toilet paper (leave several extra rolls)

Kitchen Amenities

A well-stocked kitchen allows guests to prepare meals comfortably.

Aside from the basic appliances, guests enjoy:

Coffee Maker (with coffee, filters, sugar, and creamer)
Electric Kettle
Toaster
Blender

Cookware and Utensils:

Pots and Pans
Cooking Utensils (spatulas, spoons, ladles)
Knives and Cutting Board
Measuring Cups and Spoons
Mixing Bowls
Baking Sheets and Dishes

Dinnerware:

Plates and Bowls
Glasses and Mugs
Silverware
Wine Glasses
Serving Dishes

Extras:

Basic Pantry Items (salt, pepper, cooking oil, spices)
Dish Soap and Sponges
Dish Towels
Paper Towels
Trash Bags (always leave extra—you want people to be able to get rid of their trash)
Napkins
Water Filter or Bottled Water

Safety items to have on property

Smoke and Carbon Monoxide Detectors
First Aid Kit
Fire Extinguisher

Bedroom Amenities

Creating a restful and inviting sleeping environment is key.

Blackout Curtains or Blinds
Bedside Tables and Lamps
Closet or Clothing Rack with Hangers
Dresser or Storage Space
Full-Length Mirror
Alarm Clock
Laundry Basket
Charging Stations or Accessible Outlets

Living Area Amenities

A cozy and functional living space enhances relaxation.

Smart TV with Streaming Services (Netflix, Hulu, etc.)
Cable or Satellite TV
Books and Magazines
Board Games and Cards
Bluetooth Speaker or Sound System
Throw Blankets and Cushions
Local Guidebooks and Maps
House Manual with Important Information

Laundry Facilities

Convenient laundry options are highly valued, especially for longer stays.

Laundry Detergent and Fabric Softener
Iron and Ironing Board

Outdoor Amenities

If applicable, outdoor spaces can greatly enhance the guest experience.

Outdoor Seating and Table
Grill/Barbecue with Tools
Outdoor Lighting
Gardening/Landscaping

Outdoor Heater or Fire Pit
Bicycle Storage or Provided Bicycles

Family-Friendly Amenities

Catering to families can broaden your guest base.

Crib or Pack 'n Play
High Chair
Children's Dinnerware
Toys and Games for Various Ages
Baby Bath and Changing Table
Childproofing Supplies (outlet covers, cabinet locks)
Stroller
Books for Children

Business Traveler Amenities

Appeal to business travelers with these thoughtful additions.

Dedicated Workspace or Desk
Fast and Reliable Wi-Fi
Printer and Paper
Office Supplies (pens, notepads, stapler)

Extra Touches

Small details can make a big difference in guest satisfaction.

Welcome Basket (snacks, bottled water, local treats)
Coffee and Tea Selection
Basic Medical Supplies (pain relievers, band-aids)
Umbrellas
Backup Supplies (batteries, light bulbs, fuses)

By ensuring your property is equipped with these amenities and features, you can provide a comfortable and memorable experience for your guests, encouraging positive reviews and repeat bookings. Tailor this checklist to suit your property's specific location, size, and target audience for optimal results.

Lesson 15: Buying Under a Corporate Entity

Why Use a Corporate Entity?

As I mentioned, we purchased this investment property (and the ones Eric owned before) under a corporate name, specifically an LLC (Limited Liability Company). Buying as an LLC or corporation offers several benefits that can be advantageous for real estate investors. Here are some of the key benefits:

1. Limited Liability Protection

Personal Asset Protection: When you purchase a property under a corporate name, your personal assets are generally protected from legal actions related to the property. If the property is sued or incurs debts, only the assets of the corporation or LLC are at risk, not your personal belongings like your home. This being said, I think it's important to also get liability insurance (or an umbrella policy) for properties in your corporation; it's a personal choice, but it seems like society is a little more litigious every day, and it's best to be protected.

2. Tax Advantages

Pass-Through Taxation: In an LLC, you can make a subchapter S election. This means that profits and losses can be passed through to your personal income without facing corporate taxes, which can help you avoid double taxation.

Deductible Expenses: Corporations can deduct a wide range of business expenses, including mortgage interest, property management fees, insurance, and repairs, which can reduce your overall taxable income. I'm not a lawyer or accountant, but I also recommend you take a moment and look up section 179 of the tax code, as it may benefit you in providing a write off for startup expenses for your corporation (imagine being able to purchase equipment for your company such as a computer or even a vehicle, and being able to write them off 100% on your taxes).

3. Enhanced Credibility and Professionalism

Business Entity Perception: Owning property under a corporate name can enhance your credibility and professionalism as a real estate investor, especially when dealing with lenders, tenants, and other business partners.

Branding and Marketing: Operating under a corporate name allows you to establish a brand, which can be particularly useful if you plan to scale your real estate business or manage multiple properties.

4. Simplified Ownership Transfer

Ease of Transfer: Transferring ownership of a property held by a corporation or LLC can be simpler than transferring a personally owned property. You can sell or transfer shares in the corporation or membership interests in the LLC without the need to re-title the property, which can be advantageous in estate planning or when selling a stake in the property. This was the plan with the LLC for Eric. He was too young to be part of it when he was under 18, but transferring it to him now that he's older is simple.

Estate Planning: Holding property in a corporate entity can make it easier to manage and distribute assets as part of your estate, potentially reducing probate costs and complications. Corporations and LLCs also provide a structured way to plan for the future of your real estate investment business, including succession planning and continued operation after the your involvement ends.

5. Separation of Personal and Business Finances

Clear Financial Separation: Purchasing property under a corporate name allows you to keep your personal and business finances separate, which simplifies accounting and makes it easier to track income, expenses, and profits related to your real estate investments. I have always enjoyed this separation of finances and accounts. It allows me to see clearly just what the properties are doing in terms of income and expenses.

Simplified Bookkeeping: By maintaining a clear distinction between personal and business assets, you can streamline your bookkeeping processes and ensure that all income and expenses are properly accounted for.

By utilizing the advantages of purchasing property under a corporate name, you can protect your personal assets, maximize tax benefits, and position your real estate investments for long-term success.

Since we're speaking of corporations and taxes, here are 25 things you may be able to write off as short-term rental expenses:

1. Mortgage Interest

2. Property Taxes

3. Insurance Premiums

- Deduct the cost of homeowners insurance, liability insurance, and short-term rental insurance.

4. Depreciation

- Deduct the depreciation of the property's structure, appliances, and furniture over time.

5. Property Management Fees

6. Cleaning and Maintenance

- Deduct costs for cleaning services between guest stays and routine maintenance.

7. Repairs

- Deduct expenses for repairs made to the property, such as fixing a leaky roof or replacing broken appliances.

- Consider also improvements such as adding an electronic lock to the front door, as things such as those would be deductible too.

8. Utilities

- Deduct the cost of utilities, including electricity, water, gas, internet, and cable.

9. Supplies

- Deduct the cost of supplies for guests, such as toiletries, cleaning supplies, and kitchen essentials.

10. Furniture and Appliances

- Deduct the cost of purchasing or replacing furniture, appliances, and electronics used in the rental.

11. Advertising and Marketing

- Deduct expenses for promoting your Airbnb, including listing fees on platforms like Airbnb or Vrbo, professional photography, and marketing materials.

12. Homeowners Association (HOA) Fees

- Deduct any HOA fees paid if the rental property is part of an association.

13. Legal and Professional Fees

- Deduct fees paid for legal advice, accounting, or tax preparation related to the rental.

14. Travel Expenses

- Deduct travel expenses incurred when traveling to the property for business purposes, such as maintenance or management.

15. Security System

- Deduct the cost of installing and maintaining a security system for the rental property.

16. Landscaping and Yard Care

- Deduct expenses related to lawn care, landscaping, and snow removal.

17. Licenses and Permits

- Deduct the cost of any licenses or permits required to operate the short-term rental.

18. Technology and Software

- Deduct the cost of technology or software used to manage bookings, guest communications, and property operations.

19. Home Office

- Deduct a portion of your home office expenses if you use a portion of your home exclusively for managing the rental property.

20. Professional Services

- Deduct fees for professional services such as pest control, pool maintenance, or chimney sweeping.

21. Mortgage Points

- Deduct points paid on a mortgage when financing the purchase or refinance of the rental property.

22. Home Improvements

- Deduct improvements that are capitalized and depreciated over time, such as a new roof or HVAC system.

23. Bank Fees

- Deduct bank fees related to managing rental income, such as wire transfer fees or account maintenance fees.

24. Educational Expenses

- Deduct the cost of courses, books, or seminars related to improving your short-term rental business.

25. Guest Amenities

- Deduct the cost of providing additional amenities for guests, such as welcome baskets, coffee, or extra linens.

Lesson 16: Successful Marketing and then Selling

Short-term rental advertising

What good is all the work you've done if no one sees your short-term rental? Successful marketing is key. You'll want to create a listing that stands out. You know from looking online at listings yourself that a bright professional photo and catchy description is much more attention grabbing than a dark photo clearly taken by an amateur. Don't underestimate the importance of high-quality photos, a detailed description, and highlighting unique features that appeal to travelers.

Photographers can be expensive, but I have found some inexpensive ones by searching online for "real estate photographers near me." Look through a few of the listings that come up in your area and you may be able to find a full photography package with a professional photographer and color adjusted photos for between $150-$200. It's well worth the price for the quality in my opinion.

When advertising your short-term rental, also keep in mind:

- **Pricing Strategies**:

    Maximize occupancy while ensuring profitability by pricing the property properly. There are dynamic pricing tools on the various short-term rental platforms that adjust rates based on demand and competition. Also, when there are specific event weekends, be sure to manually search the pricing of other rentals in your area to ensure that you're priced properly.

- **Guest Experience**:

    Delivering a great guest experience will go a long way toward great reviews and future bookings. Communication has been the most reliable way of ensuring guest happiness. In the game day rental, we left a notebook that Eric compiled that provided a list of his favorite restaurants (and what his favorite dishes were there). I think guests enjoyed the inside information on the best places to eat and drink. Also, I always messaged the guests to ensure that they knew that we were looking forward to their visit, commented on the game they were coming to see, provided my cell phone number and Eric's as well, and I always tried to have their favorite coffee or creamer on-site. Sometimes it's the small touches that make people feel the most cared for.

- **Ask for the Review**

  On these short-term rental platforms, reviews are everything. You need a 5-star review, so ask for it! I was upfront with guests, and I asked them to provide the 5-star review and they came through. Every single review we received on the game day home was a 5-star review except for one (which was a 4-star review). If people know what you need from them, and why you need it, they'll try to give it to you. I had some guests provide a 5-star review and then tell me privately about a minor items they thought could be improved, which I greatly appreciated.

  Here's an example of the message I would send guests at checkout:
  Hi Tristan! I hope you had a wonderful stay, and enjoyed the game! I really hope that you guys enjoyed the house and that the house earned a 5-star review. We only have a few bookings a year (just home game day weekends really) so it really means a lot to us.
  Have a save trip home and Thank you again!! 💕

Selling the Property

A few months before Eric's graduation we placed the property on the market for sale. Having professional photographs comes in handy here as well, of course. In this case, I contacted the Realtor who we had originally worked with 3 years prior for the home purchase. She sent her own professional photographer, which was a condition of the listing, and our listing immediately presented better than many of the others where the Realtor took photos with their cell phone camera.

Since the property had been a rental with a great history with the city and the zoning board, we were able to advertise it as a traditional home sale, but we were also able to promote and advertise it as an income generating short-term rental. This provided an additional level of exposure since we could be promoted to investors who wanted to purchase a property with proven rental history and that was ready to take over easily.

We sold the home to buyers who did intend to utilize it as a short-term rental as well. This worked out perfectly because we negotiated a price for the furnishings, linens, cookware…everything except for Eric's personal items essentially. This meant that we were able to stay in the home through graduation, then essentially clean up, drop off the key, and not even have to pack a U-Haul. It was extremely convenient.

When we purchased the home 3 years prior, we paid $215,000. We generated income throughout those years with the rentals, and then sold the home for $262,000.

It was a nice accomplishment to be able to have Eric live in a home for 3 years and, rather than pay out money in rent to someone else's mortgage, we were using rental income to pay down the mortgage on the house. And, the house went up in value significantly.

It all started with a change in mindset and recognizing a need that could be filled in the area.

You: How You Can Start

- **Getting Started with Short-term Rentals**: Shorter stay locations can offer higher income due to the higher per-night rates. Research areas that could benefit from a short-term rental that you could invest in.

- **Overcoming Fear of Far Away Investments**: It might seem intimidating to purchase a property that isn't in your hometown, but don't let this stop you. A great property manager can help handle things on your behalf. You can choose to buy in an area that you love to visit and rent it out while you're not there. Just be sure to follow the tax regulations for occupancy so that you can legally and properly write off your expenses.

- **Identify Opportunities in College Towns**: Focus on location, proximity to the campus, and the demand for rental during big events like graduations, sports games, and college visits.

- **Think Through Alternatives:** College-aged students may only think about housing in the same way they see their peers doing it—renting apartments or occasionally houses with friends. Sometimes just providing the idea that they can try to own a condo or house, and then rent it out to their friends (or as a short-term rental as we did), could start a conversation that leads to investing and making money on their investment by the time they graduate rather than simply spending money on rent with nothing to show for it at the end.

- **Help with Research and Negotiations**: It takes time and patience to research things like potential income from roommates or short-term rental rates. College-aged students are notoriously busy, so you may be able to spend an afternoon online and help them with some of the legwork. If they do buy a property, then you can give them a few pointers to help with negotiations. For example, Eric didn't realize at the time that you can negotiate a listing agreement in terms of commission rate and also responsibilities (like requiring that the Realtor have a professional photographer take photos of the listing). Your experience can help show younger investors where they can make money, save money, or get more for their money.

Chapter 5
The Graduate

**Constructing a Legacy.
Securing Your Family's Wealth for
the Next Generation**

Chapter 5: Constructing a Legacy.
Securing Your Family's Wealth for the Next Generation

At this point, Eric has graduated and, after a short time staying at home to secure the job he wanted, he's ready to move on and into the world and into a home of his own as an adult. However, there are still a few lessons I'd like to pass along to him, in order to ensure that he can maximize his equity and future profitability.

Additionally, I want him to deal in real estate with the future in mind. I have made many purchases and sales that I have later come to find out that I could have structured differently. My lack of knowledge in structuring and planning cost me a lot of money in taxes which I could have avoided if I knew the rules of the game. It was not knowing that cost me, and I'd like for him to avoid making those same mistakes and plan properly for the long term.

Legacy planning, and being strategic, is a crucial step in the journey of building wealth and financial independence. It's not just about accumulating assets, but also about ensuring that the next generation is prepared to manage and grow that wealth.

In this chapter, we'll go through some tax strategies and benefits that you can utilize in order to ensure that your earnings stay with your family, and your legacy, as much as possible. There's a great quote by Robert Kiyosaki that states,

"It's not how much money you make, but how much money you keep, how hard it works for you, and how many generations you keep it for."

I hope that the information in this chapter will help you as you plan for that process.

Lesson 17: House Hacking

The next step in Eric's real estate journey is house hacking. House hacking is one way for first-time home buyers looking to begin to generate wealth, and cash flow. Here's how it works: you purchase a property, live in one part of it, and rent out the other parts to help cover your mortgage. This property could be a duplex, triplex, or it could be a single-family home with extra rooms to rent. With house hacking, you reduce your housing costs while gaining rental income, making it easier to pay off your mortgage and also build equity faster than you would by just living in the home alone.

For a first-time buyer, this strategy can be a monumental game changer. Imagine buying a duplex where you live in one unit and rent out the other. You should be able to obtain owner-occupied financing (which typically has a lower interest rate than what you pay for purchasing investment property). The rent from your tenant can significantly reduce your monthly housing expenses, possibly even covering your mortgage entirely. You're essentially living for free or close to it, all while building home equity. That equity can be leveraged later for another property purchase, or you can move out of that duplex after a given time (for example some loans may require that you live in the property for at least a year to comply with the lending requirements for the owner-occupied financing) and rent out both sides of the property while you move on to the next home.

House hacking is a great way to start your investment journey.

Imagine, for example, buying a triplex as your first home. You can live in one unit and rent out the other two sides of the triplex. Not only could the rent from the other units cover your entire mortgage, but you could also have extra cash each month, which you can save for future investments. After a few years, sell the property at a profit, using the equity you've built to buy a larger home, and continue investing. The key here is that house hacking can allow you to start generating wealth from day one, even as first-time buyers.

House hacking is also a great way to learn the ropes of property management without overwhelming yourself. You'll start small, with just a few tenants, and you can grow your portfolio as you gain experience. It's a low-risk way to get started with real estate investing while still meeting your own need for housing. Plus, many lenders offer favorable terms for owner-occupied properties, making it easier to qualify for a mortgage, even if you're a first-time buyer.

Right now, Eric's plan is to start house hacking with the home he hopes to buy here in Central Florida. He's found a great house, and we're trying to negotiate with the bank. It's a bank owned foreclosure, which needs a good amount of work, but he's not afraid of the renovation and could gain a good amount of "sweat equity" by doing a lot of the work himself over time. He plans on having some of his lifelong friends live in the house with him. They would pay rent at a rate less than what they could find elsewhere, and Eric will benefit from having their rental income help pay the mortgage and utilities.

Lesson 18: Capital Gains and Your Primary Residence

I have told Eric that once he does buy the home, he should hold on to it for at least two years. The reason for doing this is to utilize a tax benefit. As I mentioned earlier, not knowing tax laws has cost me a significant amount, and I hope to help him (and you) avoid these same issues where I can.

Why is it a smart financial decision to hold on to the house for at least two years?

Because if you've lived in the home for at least two of the last five years before the sale, you can benefit from a significant tax break on the capital gains. According to the current tax laws, you can exclude up to $250,000 of the gain from the sale if you're single, and up to $500,000 if you're married filing jointly. This means you won't pay capital gains taxes on that portion of your profit.

So, if you buy a house for $250,000, and the value of that home increases to $400,000 over the next two years, you'll have a gain of $150,000. If you have lived in the home as your primary residence for two years, then that $150,000 is yours without any capital gains tax! However, let's say you sell the home just short of 2 years of ownership. Let's say you owned it for 1 year and 11 months. Then you would have to pay capital gains tax on that $150,000. Right now, a single person reporting over $50,000 income per year would have to pay 15% of that profit in taxes. That's $22,500! For a one-month difference in the date of the sale.

Can you see how knowing the tax laws and rules help you save money?

The law that allows this is known as the Capital Gains Tax Exclusion on Primary Residences, and it's covered under IRS Section 121. According to the IRS Website:

Qualifying for the exclusion

In general, to qualify for the Section 121 exclusion, you must meet both the ownership test and the use test. You're eligible for the exclusion if you have owned and used your home as your main home for a period aggregating at least two years out of the five years prior to its date of sale. You can meet the ownership and use tests during different 2-year periods. However, you

133

must meet both tests during the 5-year period ending on the date of the sale. Generally, you're not eligible for the exclusion if you excluded the gain from the sale of another home during the two-year period prior to the sale of your home. Refer to <u>Publication 523</u> *for the complete eligibility requirements, limitations on the exclusion amount, and exceptions to the two-year rule.*

(Source: <u>Topic no. 701, Sale of your home | Internal Revenue Service (irs.gov)</u>)

This exclusion applies to homeowners who have used the property as their primary residence for at least two years. So, even if your property has increased significantly in value over that time, you get to keep those profits tax-free, as long as you meet the residency requirement.

As another example, let's say you bought a home for $300,000 and after living there for two years, you sell it for $400,000. Normally, you'd have to pay capital gains tax on that $100,000 profit, but if the home was your primary residence and you meet the criteria, you could avoid paying taxes on that profit entirely. This exemption allows you to grow your wealth through real estate without the burden of extra taxes eating into your profits.

Holding the property for at least two years also gives you a buffer to ride out any fluctuations in the real estate market. It allows you more time to build equity through property appreciation and mortgage payments. Additionally, if you invest in making improvements to your home during this time, you can increase its value even more, leading to higher potential profits when you do decide to sell.

In summary, the two-year rule for capital gains tax exemption on primary residences is a huge benefit for homeowners. Not only do you get to avoid taxes on a substantial amount of profit, but it also provides flexibility, time to build equity, and the potential to maximize your returns. You can learn more about this rule directly from the IRS website, be sure to look for Publication 523. Knowing the rules can help you save money for sure!

The idea that I've presented to Eric is that he should buy a fixer upper, live in it and fix it, and sell it two years later, earning the profits tax free. He can then repeat that and keep earning and "moving up" in homes with tax free money.

Lesson 19: 1031 Exchange

Another tool to be aware of in building long term wealth is the 1031 exchange. This strategy, outlined in the U.S. tax code, allows you to defer capital gains taxes when you sell an investment property, provided you reinvest the proceeds into another like-kind property. The key benefit here is that instead of paying taxes on your profits immediately, you can use the full amount to buy a bigger or more lucrative property, which can increase your wealth over time.

One of the best parts of a 1031 exchange is that it gives you the ability to "trade up." You can sell a smaller property and use the proceeds to buy a larger one (or multiple properties), or one that generates more income, all without having to worry about paying capital gains taxes right away. This ability to keep your money working for you can help grow your real estate portfolio much faster than if you were paying taxes with every sale.

Let's go through this as an example so that we can see how it would play out in real life.

Imagine that you bought a rental property for $200,000. Time passes and you're ready to sell the unit and now it's valued at $400,000. Way to go! Now, you have a tax bill based on the $200,000 profit, which eats into that profit significantly. So, you end up with less than $400,000 to invest in on future projects (due to the taxes you had to pay). But with a 1031 exchange, you can reinvest that *entire $400,000* into a new property, deferring the taxes. Over time, this helps you increase your buying power, because every dollar stays in the market instead of going to taxes.

Another advantage of the 1031 exchange is that you can use it repeatedly. As long as you continue reinvesting in like-kind properties, you can keep deferring taxes over and over again--indefinitely. This opens up the opportunity to grow a substantial real estate portfolio without the burden of paying capital gains taxes every time you sell. And because real estate generally appreciates over time, you're building wealth on a tax-deferred basis. This is a huge benefit and yet another strategy that shows that we need to take our time to learn the rules of the game when it comes to strategizing with real estate investments and taxes.

There's also an important estate planning benefit to the 1031 exchange. If you continue using this strategy throughout your life and pass your properties to your heirs, they may inherit the properties with a "stepped-up basis." This means the property's value *at the time of your passing* becomes the new basis for capital gains calculations, potentially eliminating any deferred taxes entirely.

I have carried out a 1031 exchange once in my investing career, and I wish I had been more disciplined and utilized it more often. The process was pretty straightforward and made easier due to the requirement to use a professional in the process. Here's an overview of how it works:

Carrying out a 1031 exchange involves a series of important steps, and it's essential to follow them carefully to ensure you qualify for the tax benefits. The first step is to sell your current investment property, but before you do that, you need to identify a Qualified Intermediary (QI). The QI is a third party that handles the exchange of funds between the sale of your current property and the purchase of the new one. You cannot touch the proceeds from the sale; the QI takes control to ensure the transaction qualifies under IRS rules.

I used a large established company to handle the process, and I would recommend that you search online for a reputable company to handle yours as well.

Next, you have to meet the time requirement, which includes two specific deadlines. First, you have 45 days from the sale of your property to identify potential "replacement properties". It's essential to put together a list of up to three properties you're considering, though there are exceptions if you're dealing with high-value properties. Once identified, you then have 180 days from the sale of your original property to close on the purchase of your replacement property. Missing either of these deadlines disqualifies the exchange, so time management is critical!

Now, 180 days is a generous amount of time, so you shouldn't have any problem meeting the deadline. Just don't procrastinate.

Another key requirement is that the property you buy must be like-kind to the one you sold. This doesn't mean it has to be exactly the same type of property, but it does need to be real estate held for investment or business purposes, not personal use. For example, you could sell a rental property and exchange it for an office building or a piece of land, as long as both are considered investment properties. According to the IRS,

"Properties are of like-kind if they're of the same nature or character, even if they differ in grade or quality."

It's also important to remember that to fully defer your capital gains taxes, you need to reinvest all of the proceeds from the sale into the new property. If you choose to keep part of the money or trade down to a less expensive property, you may face a partial tax liability, referred to as "boot." So, make sure the value of the property you're buying is equal to or greater than the one you sold.

Again, while the process may seem complex, it's critical to work with professionals such as real estate attorneys, tax advisors, or companies who specialize in 1031 exchanges. They can guide you through the requirements, help ensure compliance with IRS rules, and maximize the benefits of your exchange. These professionals, along with your Qualified Intermediary, will keep the transaction smooth and ensure you don't face unnecessary taxes or penalties. It really was relatively simple when I went through the process and the company that I worked with made sure to give me a timeline, guidelines, and ensured that everything was on track.

By using the 1031 exchange, you've deferred taxes and benefited from appreciation on a more valuable property, which can further boost your investment portfolio.

Lesson 20: Opportunity Zones

Opportunity Zones were created as part of the Tax Cuts and Jobs Act of 2017 to encourage long-term investments in economically distressed areas. These zones were designated by state governors and then certified by the U.S. Department of the Treasury. The goal of the program was to provide an incentive for investors to put capital into these areas by offering tax benefits, which, in turn, should help stimulate economic growth, create jobs, and uplift communities that had been struggling.

For real estate investors, these Opportunity Zones present a unique opportunity to defer and potentially *eliminate* capital gains taxes. Did you see that? Potentially *eliminate* capital gains taxes all together on the project.

Here's how it works. If an investor reinvests capital gains from the sale of another asset into a qualified Opportunity Zone fund within 180 days, they can defer the taxes on those gains until 2026. Moreover, if they hold the investment for at least 10 years, any additional appreciation on the new Opportunity Zone property is completely tax-free.

I have not yet personally benefited from an Opportunity Zone project, but I'm actively working to find a property in an opportunity zone to buy so that I can utilize this tax benefit.

Opportunity Zones are a powerful tool for long-term real estate investing. Not only do investors have the chance to grow their portfolio in emerging areas, but they also receive substantial tax benefits along the way. Imagine purchasing a property in an Opportunity Zone that rapidly appreciates in value. After holding it for 10 years, you can sell it and not pay any taxes on the increase in value. That kind of tax savings can be huge, and again, it comes from learning and knowing the rules and benefits of investing strategically.

Separately from the purely financial aspect, Opportunity Zones also give investors the chance to leave a lasting legacy. By investing in areas that need revitalization, real estate investors can make a significant impact on the community while simultaneously growing their wealth. Renovating properties or building new ones in these zones can create jobs, increase property values, and improve the overall quality of life for residents. Leasing the units via section 8 or HSN programs could help needy tenants find good housing, and provide steady government backed rental income. As these areas improve, investors can see both social and financial returns, creating a long-lasting legacy.

However, Opportunity Zones are not a permanent feature of the tax code. Right now, the tax benefits associated with them will begin to phase out after 2026. After this period, the deferral of taxes on capital gains will no longer be available, though the potential to eliminate taxes on the appreciation of Opportunity Zone investments held for 10 years will remain intact. This makes it crucial for investors to act now if they want to take full advantage of the benefits. That's the one real caveat I have about this tax benefit, its future is uncertain. I'd still like to invest in an opportunity zone and hope that the 10-year investment benefit will remain part of the tax code.

Real estate investors can utilize Opportunity Zones not only for their tax advantages but also as a way to diversify their portfolio. These areas are often prime for growth, especially as more development and revitalization efforts take hold. By getting in early, you can benefit from rising property values, increased rents, and improved neighborhood amenities, all while keeping your eye on the long-term goal of tax-free appreciation.

So, Opportunity Zones provide a powerful incentive for real estate investors looking to create wealth while making a positive social impact. Through strategic investments in these areas, investors can defer capital gains, enjoy tax-free growth, and be part of transforming communities. It's an ideal way to combine profitable investing with meaningful legacy-building.

You: How You Can Start

- **Make money on your own residence:** If you combine strategies like house hacking and making use of the Capital Gains Tax Exclusion on Primary Residences, then you can really make your money work for you. To start with, primary residences benefit from more favorable loan terms, and lower down payment requirements. This means that you can get into a home at a lower price than you would an investment property, and you can help pay off the mortgage with rent from roommates or tenants (in the case of a duplex or triplex). After 2 years you can decide if you'd like to sell that property and keep the profit under the Capital Gains Tax Exclusion on Primary Residences, or if you want to keep that property as an income generating investment and move on to your next primary residence, again with the favorable owner-occupied loan terms.

- **Think 5 years in advance:** I know, it seems daunting, you're just focused on getting started now, not thinking about 5 years in the future. But, just as every business plan contains an exit strategy, your real estate investment plan should also have some goals and exit strategies. Learn about the current tax laws to see what can benefit you most as you get started on your plan.

Legacy: How You Can Help Your Children or Grandchildren Start

- **Financial Education as a Legacy**: As we touched on earlier, early financial education is key to future success for young people. I hope that the amazing tax strategies and benefits outlined in this chapter has helped to show how significantly education about money and tax laws can help in the retention of wealth. And, importantly, how expensive a lesson it is when you don't know the tax laws and no one is there to help you with them. Helping the next generation to think about money when they're young can open up their minds to investing and thinking about money and assets as a tool. I have had the pleasure, and honor, of speaking at various high schools regarding real estate investing, assets, leverage, and passive income. I challenge them to think of what they would buy, or invest in, to generate passive income. It is so exciting to see how they light up once they start to think of how money can be used to generate passive cash flow in their lives, and some of the examples of passive income that they think of are quite unique. Grandparents and parents can help young people learn about the difference between assets and liabilities. Also, lifetime experience allows us to provide real world information on investing so that they learn from our experiences. This includes teaching them about saving, investing, managing money, and understanding the value of hard work and smart financial decisions. Be open with your history of homeownership and equity growth. If you don't own a home, be forthcoming in sharing how much you've paid in rent over the past 5 years, and how that payment has increased, and how you feel about that. Speaking about taxes is often more difficult, because it's something that seems so complicated to most of us, and there's so much out there that we can't possibly know. But it's important to have the conversation and to know that there are benefits and strategies that exist and that we should seek out.

Chapter 6
The Future

Some Final Thoughts to Share

The general premise of this book, and probably the reason that you picked it up, is to **Build Wealth**. But we really haven't defined what that is, and it can certainly be different for everyone.

Wealth can mean different things to different people. For some, it's having a large sum of money or assets. For others, it's about financial independence and the ability to live comfortably without worrying about money. I would define wealth as having sufficient financial resources to meet your needs and achieve your goals, both now and in the future. With that in mind, to me, building wealth successfully involves creating a sustainable and growing financial foundation. It's not about getting rich quickly, but about developing habits and strategies (and a real estate portfolio) that will provide financial security and growth over time.

There's also a legacy that exists beyond money. In part this can come through passing down values, principles, and life lessons along with financial assets to future generations. This could include philanthropy, community involvement, or family traditions. Creating passive income and a portfolio of assets can also allow you to incorporate charitable giving into your legacy planning, such as setting up a family foundation or donating to causes that are important to you and your family.

At this point we've gone over real estate investing that can set up for a baby's college education and a home for them when they are adults. We've gone through a rental renovation on a fix and flip, and we've worked on establishing a short-term rental. We've reviewed several investment techniques that you often see touted on social media and in real estate courses such as wholesaling, house hacking, and BRRRR. We've touched on using a revokable trust or setting up corporate entities for your purchases and utilizing tax benefits such as Section 179 when setting up your corporation. We've also gone through tax secrets that can help you retain your earnings, such as 1031 Exchanges, Opportunity Zones, and taking advantage of Capital Gains Exemptions on Primary Residences. These should hopefully have you excited and ready to start on your way to building an empire.

> **Let's do it together:** If you'd like to get started but don't want to go it alone, visit my website and view resources and get support.
> https://marciasocas.com/**building-wealth-resources/**

Estate Planning and Asset Protection

Once you've started, you'll want to ensure that your wealth can be passed down easily, properly, and most effectively to your future generations. In doing so, you'll want to speak with an attorney to establish a will and trust. Make sure you choose the right beneficiaries and spell out how you want things handled. Also, keep your paperwork up to date as circumstances change. For example, when my children were under age, and unable to manage a real estate portfolio, a company was named that would handle real estate assets and property management. This is something that obviously changes with time, and it'll be important to update the paperwork.

Transferring Wealth Efficiently

Transferring your wealth doesn't have to wait until after your lifetime. You can also gift assets during your lifetime, and there are other tax benefits for doing so. There are also limitations, so be sure to speak with a tax professional when you're ready to get started on that part of things.

Life insurance can also be a valuable tool in legacy planning, providing a tax-free lump sum to beneficiaries and helping to cover estate taxes or other expenses.

Business Succession Planning: plan for the transfer of a family business or other investments, ensuring a smooth transition and continued success.

DIYing your Real Estate Empire

There is no doubt that you need professionals that will help you on your way to building your real estate empire. However, no one is going to care about it more than you do. I say this because I've had personal experiences where I've relied on professionals and yet they haven't fully protected our investments. I'll give you two brief examples.

The first was after we sold a commercial building as well as a long term rental which had a good deal of equity in it. Selling both of those properties caused us to have a really high tax bill that year. Our accountant prepared our tax returns and presented us with the bill. It was only a year later that I realized that, if he had advised us on tax saving strategies when we had spoken with him about our sale plans, we could have invested the money in an Opportunity Zone or done a 1031 Exchange and avoided the very large tax bill we incurred. I learned that we need to make sure to use a tax professional that specializes in real estate investing, and we should have a planning meeting at the beginning of the year to properly structure any sales or investments.

The other example came after using a financial advisor. We'd used this financial advising company for years. They collected their fees every quarter, and held a virtual year end summary call at the end of the year to review their performance. Eventually, we decided to change companies because we weren't happy with the return we were receiving. It was only in a meeting with the new company that we were interviewing that I learned that it is possible to borrow against investments without having to sell them. Borrowing against them doesn't generate any capital gains or tax bill. Since our financial advisor had never advised us that this was possible, we had often sold stock (and paid taxes on the sale) in order to invest in a property. I was shocked. How had I never heard of this? Imagine how upset I was when my 'old financial advisors' told me that they could have put that in place years ago but they simply never bothered to think through or discuss our plans as investors or offer this as a suggestion. It's another example of how the experiences I've had have sometimes come as costly lessons, ones that I'd like for you to be able to avoid.

So, even though you need a team of professionals on your side, no one will ever care as much as you do about your situation. Communicate your goals with your team of professionals often, and ask them what strategies they can recommend to help you. And, always keep yourself educated so that you can advocate for yourself.

Thank you

Thank you for allowing me to share my experiences with you. I hope that the real life stories served to put the theories into concrete terms and also to show you that it can be done. So often I've read books and seen courses advertised by people who claim to be experts but who don't provide any actual proof of their experiences. They often tout hypothetical stories and conversations with perfect endings.

Investing in real estate has not been perfect. I've lost out on some opportunities on the way, and paid more in taxes several times, but I certainly can't complain. Real estate investing has created a stream of passive income that has allowed me to pursue what I truly love.

I love finding a deal, fixing it up, and creating something beautiful and higher in value than it was when I found it. I love sharing the "how to's" of everything, because I'd like for you to be able to do it as well. You can do this. Thank you again for allowing me to be part of your journey.

Now it's time for you to DIY your destiny!

---

*Reminder: This book comes with worksheets to help you with your investment goals, planning, analyzing property, and strategizing. These can all be downloaded, for free, at:

www.MarciaSocas.com/free-building-wealth-book-worksheets

How a young investor can start

Establishing an empire in real estate investing, especially as a young investor, requires a combination of strategic planning, continuous learning, and smart decision-making. Here's a step-by-step guide to help young investors build a strong foundation and scale their real estate portfolio into an empire:

1. Start with Education and Networking

- **Learn the Basics**: Before diving in, educate yourself on the fundamentals of real estate investing. Read books, attend seminars, listen to podcasts, and follow successful investors.

- **Build a Network**: Surround yourself with experienced mentors, real estate agents, brokers, and other investors. Networking can provide valuable insights, opportunities, and partnerships.

2. Set Goals

- Establish short-term and long-term goals. For example, aim to acquire one rental property per year or flip a certain number of houses by a specific time frame.

3. Start Small, but Think Big

- **Buy Your First Rental Property**: Start with a single property, such as a small rental or a fixer-upper. Use this as a learning experience to understand the ins and outs of property management, renovation, and tenant relations.

- **House Hacking**: Consider house hacking. This strategy helps cover your mortgage and builds equity while giving you hands-on experience.

4. Use Leverage to your Advantage

- **Use Leverage**: Take advantage of mortgages to maximize your buying power. Leverage allows you to control more assets with less of your own money, accelerating portfolio growth.

- **Understand Financing Options**: Explore different financing options such as conventional loans, FHA loans, hard money loans, or even partnerships with other investors.

5. Focus on Cash Flow

- **Positive Cash Flow Properties**: Always prioritize properties that generate positive cash flow. This means the income from the property exceeds all expenses, providing a steady stream of income.

- **Build a Reserve Fund**: Set aside a portion of your rental income for unexpected expenses, repairs, and vacancies to ensure financial stability. It's helpful to keep these funds in a separate bank account so that you're not tempted to use the money.

6. Scale Through Reinvestment

- **Reinvest Profits**: Rather than spending the profits from your investments, reinvest them into acquiring more properties. This reinvestment strategy compounds your growth over time.

- **Utilize the BRRRR Strategy**: Buy, Rehab, Rent, Refinance, Repeat (BRRRR) is a powerful method to scale quickly. After rehabilitating a property and renting it out, refinance it to pull out equity, then use that equity to buy your next property.

7. Utilize Tax Laws

- **Learn and Plan:** Learn which tax laws exist and that you can benefit from when selling and reinvesting. Make sure your know about section 179 benefits when establishing your business, the capital gains exclusion on primary residences, 1031 Exchanges, and Opportunity Zones.

8. Embrace Technology and Management Tools

- **Property Management Software**: Use technology to manage your properties efficiently, including rent collection, maintenance requests, and tenant communication.

- **Market Analysis Tools**: Leverage tools for market analysis to identify high-potential investment areas and track market trends.

9. Protect Your Assets

- **Legal Structure**: Set up your real estate investments under an LLC or other appropriate legal entity to protect your personal assets and take advantage of tax benefits.

- **Insurance**: Ensure all properties are adequately insured to protect against losses from disasters, liability claims, or other risks.

10. Continuously Educate and Adapt

- **Stay Informed**: The real estate market is constantly evolving. Stay up-to-date on market trends, new laws, and emerging investment strategies. Don't wait for the perfect market to buy real estate, but know whether you're in a buyer's market or seller's market so that you can negotiate most effectively.

- **Adapt to Changes**: Be flexible and ready to adapt your strategy as market conditions change. Whether it's shifting to short-term rentals during a high tourism season or selling off underperforming properties, adaptability is key.

11. Build a Strong Team

- **Assemble a Team of Experts**: As you scale, you'll need a solid team including a real estate agent, property manager, accountant, attorney, and contractors. A reliable team will help you manage your growing portfolio efficiently.

- **Outsource Where Needed**: Don't hesitate to outsource property management or other tasks as your portfolio grows. This allows you to focus on acquiring more properties and scaling your business.

12. Focus on Legacy Planning

- **Think Long-Term**: As you build your empire, consider the long-term legacy you want to leave. Plan for succession and how your investments will be managed or passed on to future generations.

- **Educate the Next Generation**: If you intend to pass on your empire to your children or family, start educating them early on the principles of real estate investing.

13. Be Patient and Persistent

- **Patience Pays Off**: Real estate investing is a long-term game. Don't rush into deals—carefully analyze each opportunity to ensure it aligns with your strategy.

- **Persistence**: There will be challenges along the way, from bad tenants to market downturns. Persistence and a problem-solving mindset will keep you moving forward. There are lots of unexpected twists along the way, but you can face them and overcome them. Keep thinking creatively and remember that when you own the real estate you own the asset and that's your strength.

The Worksheets

Here is the list of the free worksheets, included with the book, created to help you:

Goal Setting Worksheet
Property Evaluation Checklist
Investment Analysis Worksheet
Financing Options Comparison Sheet
Renovation Budget Planner
Property Management Checklist
Deal Comparison Worksheet
Monthly Cash Flow Tracker
Tax Deduction Tracker
1031 Exchange Worksheet
Exit Strategy Worksheet
Legacy Planning Worksheet

As these sheets are designed to be printed on letter size paper, they're available to you as a free download at:

www.MarciaSocas.com/free-building-wealth-book-worksheets

Chapter 7

Appendix and Resources

Questions people often ask me as a Realtor

1. How much can I afford? Most lenders suggest that your monthly mortgage payment (including taxes and insurance) shouldn't exceed 28% of your gross monthly income. Don't be afraid to call a lender for a pre-qualification, it'll take about 15 minutes on the phone and will give you a clearer picture based on your income, debt, and expenses (before they need to pull your credit).

2. What credit score do I need to buy a house? A credit score of 620 or higher is typically required to qualify for a conventional loan. However, programs like FHA loans are available for buyers with lower scores, sometimes as low as 580.

3. How much do I need for a down payment? Many people believe they need 20% down, but that's not always the case. Depending on the loan program, you can buy with as little as 3% to 5% down. FHA loans, for example, require only 3.5%. Plus, there are down payment assistance programs for first-time buyers. Explore your options!

4. What's included in closing costs? Closing costs typically range from 2% to 5% of the home's purchase price. I'll provide a breakdown in the next section.

5. How long does it take to buy a home? The process of buying a home can take anywhere from a few weeks to a few months. It depends on how long it takes to find a home, secure financing, and close on the deal.

6. How can I increase my credit score? The quickest way to improve your credit is to focus on a few key actions. First, pay down existing credit card balances to reduce your credit utilization rate, which has a big impact on your score. Next, pay your bills on time—setting up automatic payments can help with this. If you have any errors on your credit report, dispute them immediately to have them corrected. Don't open new credit accounts or make large purchases that could increase your debt.

7. Can I negotiate price with builders? Typically, in a builder community, you can't negotiate the price because that will affect future appraisals. However, get creative and ask the builder to pay some of your closing costs, loan points, or provide extra design center credits.

Closing costs

In chapter 1 I mentioned closing costs and promised to tell you a little more about them, for those who aren't experienced with them already. When you purchase a property, you will have costs associated with that purchase. Some come from the act of obtaining a mortgage, others have to do with paying the government (local or state), and others have to do with local customs and requirements (such as using a title agency or real estate attorney for the closing). While the fees will vary somewhat from area to area, here's a general overview:

If this is your first time hearing about closing fees, this is a lot but don't get overwhelmed, we can get through these and find a way to pay for them.

Bank fees:
You'll be charged some fees by the **bank** or lender that is giving you the loan.
These fees can include:
Processing fee
Origination fee
Underwriting fee
Appraisal fee
Credit Report fee
Discount points

Governmental fees:
You'll also typically have some fees charged by the **government** for recording your new note and mortgage, and the sale in general. These fees are typically seen as:
Intangible tax
Note tax
Transfer tax
Recording fee

Title company fees:

Then, there's the **title company (or attorney)** who prepares the documents for closing and carries out the closing process. Their fees may include:
Closing fee
Title search fee
Title insurance fees
Lien search fee
Courier fee
Survey

Association fees:

If the home you're buying is in a homeowner's association or condo association, then there may be a:
HOA initiation fee

Fees for Reserves:

And, as if those weren't enough to intimidate you, you may also have escrow reserves. These are payments that you pay in advance. They're not fees but rather amounts that the bank collects on your behalf to use when you need them. These typically include:

Property tax
Homeowner's Insurance

Real Estate fees:

You may also have to pay your real estate agent fee.

It's ok to feel overwhelmed. It's not ok to let that stop you.

Your lender or real estate agent will go over these fees with you. If you can, try to see if the seller will cover some of these fees for you as that will save you cash at closing.

Studies Referenced in Lesson 5: Talking about money

National Endowment for Financial Education (NEFE) Study:

- National Endowment for Financial Education. "The Impact of Financial Education on Financial Literacy and Financial Behaviors." https://www.nefe.org/

Council for Economic Education Report:

- Council for Economic Education. *Survey of the States: Economic and Personal Finance Education in Our Nation's Schools.* New York: Council for Economic Education, 2020. https://www.councilforeconed.org/

Brookings Institution Study:

- Elliott, William, and Melinda Lewis. "The Link Between Financial Literacy and Behavior." *Brookings Institution*, 2015. brookings.edu.

Jump$tart Coalition Findings:

- Jump$tart Coalition. "Financial Literacy and the Impact on Future Financial Behaviors." Jumpstart.org

T. Rowe Price's Parents, Kids & Money Survey:

- T. Rowe Price. *Parents, Kids & Money Survey.* 2020. troweprice.gcs-web.com/news-releases/news-release-details/t-rowe-price-recommends-families-talk-their-kids-about-finances

FINRA Investor Education Foundation Research:

- FINRA Investor Education Foundation. "Financial Capability in the United States." 2019. Finra.org

Global Financial Literacy Excellence Center (GFLEC) Study:

- Lusardi, Annamaria, and Olivia S. Mitchell. "The Economic Importance of Financial Literacy: Theory and Evidence." *Global Financial Literacy Excellence Center (GFLEC),* 2014. www.nber.org/papers/w18952

Sources used for ROI on home renovations:

Garage Door Replacement ROI:

- Fixr. "Cost vs Value 2024: Curb Appeal Projects Bring Highest ROIs." Fixr.com. Accessed August 2024. https://www.fixr.com.

Minor Kitchen Remodel ROI:

- Builder Magazine. "The 2024 Cost vs. Value Report Proves 'Curb Appeal' Still Drives Highest Value for Remodeling Projects." BuilderOnline.com. Published April 26, 2024. Accessed August 2024. https://www.builderonline.com.

Entry Door Replacement ROI:

- Builder Magazine. "The 2024 Cost vs. Value Report Proves 'Curb Appeal' Still Drives Highest Value for Remodeling Projects." BuilderOnline.com. Published April 26, 2024. Accessed August 2024. https://www.builderonline.com.

Bathroom Remodel ROI:

- RenoFi. "The 10 Best Home Improvement ROI Projects of 2023 (According to Experts)." RenoFi.com. Accessed August 2024. https://www.renofi.com.

- Remodeling Magazine. "Cost vs. Value: Key Trends in the 2023 Cost vs. Value Report." ("Cost vs. Value | JLC Online") Remodeling.hw.net. Accessed August 2024. https://www.remodeling.hw.net.

Siding Replacement ROI:

- Builder Magazine. "The 2024 Cost vs. Value Report Proves 'Curb Appeal' Still Drives Highest Value for Remodeling Projects." ("The 2024 Cost vs. Value Report Proves 'Curb Appeal' Still Drives ...") BuilderOnline.com. Published April 26, 2024. Accessed August 2024. https://www.builderonline.com.

Let's Do It Together

For more resources, information, and connection, you can find me in the following locations:

Website:

https://www.MarciaSocas.com

On my website I have info about investing but also details about specific flip projects I've undertaken, including before and after photos, projects, and profits made.

Website with info specific to this book:

https://www.MarciaSocas.com/building-wealth-resources

Find me on Social Media here:

Instagram: www.instagram.com/marciasocas/

TikTok: www.tiktok.com/@myhomegoals

Pinterest: www.pinterest.com/marciasocas/

And don't forget the free worksheets to help you on DIYing your destiny through real estate investing. These can all be downloaded, for free, at:

www.MarciaSocas.com/free-building-wealth-book-worksheets

Other Books You May Enjoy

Find them at: www.MarciaSocas.com/books

Small Space, Big Style: *Transforming Small Spaces with DIY Renovations: Over 100 Renovation Projects, Tutorials and Tips for your Apartment, Condo, or Tiny Home*

This is a book I wrote with very detailed step-by-step instructions on renovating a property. It contains before and after photos as well as in-process pictures, materials lists, and estimated costs.

The Ultimate Renovation Project Organizer: *Over 40 pages of worksheets, tips, info, room guides, and budget sheets for your DIY Renovation*

This organizer is meant to help you plan and execute your own renovation. You can download it once and then print it out for every renovation you undertake.

Real Estate Property Info Logbook: *Store home and lease details, equipment model numbers, and loan information for your rental properties*

Once you've started investing, this journal will give you a centralized place to store information on each property. Write down your loan terms, the paint colors you used, the appliance information, the dates of renovations, all of the things that you'll want to have easily accessible when you need them.

Find them at: www.MarciaSocas.com/books

Download the Free Worksheets

These worksheets are available to you completely free for download in order to help you get started with your planning and investing:

- Goal Setting Worksheet
- Property Evaluation Checklist
- Investment Analysis Worksheet
- Financing Options Comparison Sheet
- Renovation Budget Planner
- Property Management Checklist
- Deal Comparison Worksheet
- Monthly Cash Flow Tracker
- Tax Deduction Tracker
- 1031 Exchange Worksheet
- Exit Strategy Worksheet
- Legacy Planning Worksheet

www.MarciaSocas.com/free-building-wealth-book-worksheets/